Malcolm R. Hébert's

California Brandy Drinks

"The One Bottle Bar"

PUBLISHED BY
THE WINE APPRECIATION GUILD WITH
THE CALIFORNIA BRANDY ADVISORY BOARD

Published by The Wine Appreciation Guild
1377 Ninth Avenue
San Francisco, CA 94122
(415) 566-3532

In Cooperation with The California Brandy Advisory Board
235 Montgomery Street
San Francisco, Ca 94104
(415) 398-0220

ISBN 0-932664-21-0

Library of Congress Catalog Card Number 81-51668

Printed in The United States of America

Cover Design and Illustrations: Bill Lansberg
Contributing Editors: James McManus
                      John R. Poimiroo
                      Susan Lang
                      Linda Nielsen Healey
Typography: Vera Allen Composition

Other Books Published by The Wine Appreciation Guild:
EPICUREAN RECIPES OF CALIFORNIA WINEMAKERS
THE CHAMPAGNE COOKBOOK
GOURMET WINE COOKING THE EASY WAY
FAVORITE RECIPES OF CALIFORNIA WINEMAKERS
NEW ADVENTURES IN WINE COOKERY
WINE COOKBOOK OF DINNER MENUS
EASY RECIPES OF CALIFORNIA WINEMAKERS
THE POCKET ENCYCLOPEDIA OF CALIFORNIA WINE
IN CELEBRATION OF WINE AND LIFE
WINE CELLAR RECORD BOOK
WINE IN EVERYDAY COOKING
THE CALIFORNIA WINE DRINK BOOK
THE WINE LOVERS COOKBOOK
CORKSCREWS: An Introduction to Their Appreciation

Contents

INTRODUCTION
By Malcolm R. Hébert

The first time I ever tasted California brandy was some 35 years ago. And oddly enough, it was at a French cognac tasting. I was a reporter on the "Chicago Daily News" and one afternoon, the editor got an invitation to a cognac tasting. "Here," he said, "you are from a French background; you go to the tasting."

In those days, newspaper reporters were only given invitations by their editors if the event was scheduled after working hours. I got off at five and the tasting started at seven, so I had two hours for dinner.

The tasting was held in one of Chicago's largest wine and spirits shops. Inside were seven tables, each with a different cognac. Alongside the bottles were small three ounce snifters. There was no one behind the tables, no one to tell you how to taste, and no one to tell you in which order the brandies were to be tasted.

So my first introduction to the world of tasting brandy was to pour until the snifter was half full, inhale it, swirl it around in the snifter and drink it. As I progressed from table to table, my note taking became less readable. Next to the last table was a young lady who offered me an eighth drink. It too came in a snifter. As she handed it to me, I asked, "Is this another brandy?"

"Yes," she said. "It will help smooth your palate." That's just what I needed. I inhaled, I swirled, I swallowed. The girl stared at me. I said to her, "Why do they always save the best for the last?" She showed me the bottle.

It was brandy all right, but just above the word brandy was "California."

That California brandy was the best brandy I had tasted. It not only was better than the cognacs I tasted, but the California brandy was by far the smoothest, softest and a great deal lighter. From that day on, I became a California brandy advocate.

The California brandy that I tasted 35 years ago is not the same brandy that's being distilled today. The California brandies of today are far more mature and are blended with six characteristics: bouquet, body, lightness, dryness, smoothness, and flavor. California brandy must have an aroma and flavor characteristic of the grape. It must not be dominated by oak or artificial flavors. It should first of all display an inherent grape quality; it should be light and soft to the taste, largely a result of patient ageing.

Short History of California Brandy

California brandy is America's brandy. Wine is roduced in many parts of the country, but only California produces brandy. The art of making brandy was introduced to California some 200 years ago by the Spanish mission fathers. Almost right after they arrived they established vineyards, primarily to make wine for sacramental use. But within a very short time, the fathers were making brandy for commercial purposes and by 1774, they were shipping barrels of California brandy around the Horn and back to Spain.

Before long, a few missions gained reputations as fine brandymakers, especially Father Duran, the brandymaker at Mission Santa Barbara. It was said that Father Duran made brandy that was "doubly distilled and as strong as the Reverend Father's faith." Generally, mission brandy was produced for medicinal purposes, to fortify altar wines and for the trade. In 1819, a barrel of the fine mission brandy sold for $80.

Around 1830 the missions began to decline, but as the missions disappeared, brandy was beginning to be made commercially by a few early settlers. One such man was a Frenchman from Bordeaux, Jean Louis Vignes, who established vineyards, a winery and a still in the pueblo of Los Angeles. An experienced distiller and cooper, Vignes engaged in brandy making and by 1840 was selling his brandy to many other settlements in California for as little as four dollars a gallon.

Vignes, who could be considered the "Father of California brandy," aged his brandy for years in oak casks to add to its smoothness. "When six, eight or ten years old," one observer wrote, "Vignes' brandy becomes amber, rich, an oily liquor that was very palatable."

By mid century, hundreds of settlers had established significant vineyards and were producing both wine and brandy. Among these settlers was the legendary figure of California viticulture, Agoston Haraszthy, who imported 100,000 vine cuttings from Europe "to produce not only finer wines, but better brandy."

With the Gold Rush of '49, California's population soared and demand for its brandy increased accordingly. Distilleries and vineyards burgeoned in the fertile valleys of Northern California. Even Captain John Sutter of gold discovery fame constructed a brandy distillery at Fort Sutter on the American River. California brandy had become the true drink of the West.

By the turn of the century, California brandy was being exported and had received international acclaim. These included coveted ribbons of merit at exhibitions in the brandy drinking capital of the world, Paris. Production of California brandy remained limited though, and with the advent of Prohibition, virtually stopped.

Not until the middle of the 20th century did California brandymakers realize the great potential for fine brandy in the United States. The upsurge by Americans in their appreciation of California wines helped pave the way as more people began to discover their oldest of native distilled spirits, California brandy. Today, of every five bottles of brandy consumed in the United States, four of those come from California.

America's Brandyland

A 200-mile corridor from Lodi in Northern California south to Bakersfield is the most productive agricultural region in the world. This is the San Joaquin Valley which has been named America's "brandyland."

This lush valley has just the right soil, water and climatic conditions needed to produce the proper grapes for making some of the finest brandy in the world. Few places like it exist elsewhere. The valley is bounded on the east by the snow-capped High Sierra, and on the west by the Coastal range which buffers it from cool Pacific breezes. These mountains act as a natural thermostat and as an abundant source of water. If the consistency of California brandy can be attributed to any one element, it would be this natural balance of heat and moisture, so important to the growth of ripe and sound grapes.

Careful land management enhances these natural gifts and this is the task of grape growers and vineyard keepers, most of whom represent second and third generation families.

California, over the years, has produced more than 125 varieties of grapes used for making brandy. Today, Tokay is grown in the northern area, and Thompson seedless is favored in the central and southern parts of the state. Both the Tokay and Thompson seedless are particularly fragrant and rich in sugar content which are ideal for producing a smooth, light brandy that appeals to American palates. Other grapes used for blending include Emperor, Grenache, Malaga, and Petit Sirah.

Grape varietals must be harvested at their peak condition because the quality of the grapes is critical in the making of fine brandy. Growers combine scientific methods and instinctive abilities to determine the precise moment for picking. Harvest extends from late August in the south to early October in the north.

Making of California Brandy

Three basic processes produce California brandy. These are: *fermentation* of the grapes to wine; *distillation* of the wine to brandy and the *ageing* of the young brandy into a smooth, finished product.

After the grapes are picked and crushed, the must or juice is put into large tanks. Precise amounts of yeast are added to the juice to control fermentation. It takes between three to five days for the fermentation to be completed. The wine then goes to distillation. It is not aged prior to distillation, as brandies made from aged wines do not yield the intense fragrance so characteristic of fine California brandy.

Distillation is a simple process. Wine is heated by steam to a boiling point in a closed container. The resultant vapors are collected and condensed back into a liquid state by cooling. Each element of the wine has a different boiling temperature. Elements that boil at low temperatures vaporize first. These are called the "heads." Those with the highest boiling points vaporize last. They are called "tails." Within these parts are high levels of fusel oils, aldehydes and other chemicals, which the brandymakers call "congeners."

Between the heads and the tails of the distillation is the "heart," which is used in making California brandy since it is high in alcoholic concentration and relatively low in congeners. Some congeners are retained to give the brandy its special character. If all were removed, you would have pure alcohol.

Basically, two kinds of stills are used to make brandy today, the *pot still* and the *continuous still*. The pot still dates back to the Middle Ages, while the continuous still dates back to 1830 and was invented by an Irishman named Aeneas Coffey. In fact, some people often refer to his invention as the "Coffey" still.

California brandy is made by the continuous still method because it permits better control of the product and yields a distillate of lighter body. European brandymakers use the pot still method which yields a heavier bodied product. Some California brandymakers use pot stills for blending purposes, however.

The distillate that emerges from the still is 150 to 170 proof, which is considered to be an extremely desirable concentration for achieving the fruitiness of the finished brandy. Purified water is added to the spirit lowering it to about 120 proof. It is then put into American oak barrels for ageing and just before bottling, more purified water is added to bring its strength down to about 80 proof.

Ageing California Brandy

The lightness that you and I and millions of Americans like in California brandy, is deliberately choreographed by the brandymaster to please our palates. The practice in California is to avoid those once favored heavy, tannic brandies and produce lighter, easier to drink spirits which Americans prefer. Such lightness in California brandy is obtained by the use of oak barrels that have been charred inside and which have lost some of their initial tannin by having first been used for other spirits. Casks are carefully selected by brandymasters because different oaks affect the brandies in different ways.

Ageing the spirit in wood mellows and influences the flavor of the brandy. Air, too, helps, for it permeates the barrels, which adds its own special nuance. It is here that the brandymaster must consider each barrel of brandy, choosing one for fullness, another for lightness, and another for body in making his final blends. Brandy that is between 50% and 60% alcohol responds best to oak. In dry conditions with a great deal of air circulation, some water evaporates in the barrel and the brandy becomes higher in alcoholic content. Under damp conditions, it is the alcohol that evaporates. Again the brandymaster must control these atmospheric conditions to get the optimum from the distillate and the oak.

Another fact the brandymaster must take into consideration is the size of the cask. There is more exchange between the brandy and the wood in small casks as opposed to larger casks. For California brandy, mostly white American oak barrels (Quercus alba) of seasoned wood of about 50 gallons are used.

The taste of a brandy is sometimes modified by stock held in other woods or other sized oak casks. In some cases, continuous-still brandy is blended with small amounts of pot-stilled brandy to add a certain fullness and pungency to the final product. In addition, brandies aged as long as 10 years in wood are used in the final blend, which produces a very mellow and highly aromatic brandy. Each brandymaster has a secret formula for blending his brandies and that is why tasting brandies of many kinds and styles is important in selecting those that please your palate. (See tasting brandy below.)

For many years, people associated a dark amber and deep brown color with old brandies. Indeed, 75 to 100 years ago, many European brandies were aged 25, 30, even 50 years in oak casks. They were expensive and only the wealthy could afford to store and serve them. Today, the hue of the brandy is no longer an indication of the time a brandy has slept in the wood. Small amounts of caramel, which is tasteless and in no way affects the properties of the brandy, are universally used in coloring brandy.

The ageing process of California brandy is by far the most expensive part of brandymaking. The barrel cost is high, storage is expensive and there is the ever-present problem of brandy evaporation while resting and maturing in the cask. This is why good brandy can never be cheap.

How to Taste California Brandy

Throughout my travels in the United States demonstrating the techniques of using, cooking and tasting California brandy there is one question that I am asked over and over again; "What's the best brandy?"

My stock answer is simply, "The best brandy is the brandy you like best."

That may sound like an answer straight from Madison Avenue, but it is the truth. The only way to determine just which brandies you like best is to taste them.

If you can taste food and wine, you can taste brandy, but it is a little harder. Inside your mouth you have some 10,000 taste buds. They have been educated to various foods and wines you eat and drink, what your parents served you, and what your friends have served you. What you like and dislike are a product of years of tasting experience. And because you want your taste buds to be at their peak when tasting brandy, you should taste brandy like the professionals.

The men and women who make their living sampling brandy and deciding which and what blends will be marketed to the public have a special way to taste brandy. They mix one part brandy with one part room temperature distilled water. This enables them to detect the differences in *body, bouquet, taste* and *flavor* of the various brandies.

There is no one correct taste, no one correct blend and no one correct brandy. One person's taste may favor a more full bodied brandy. Another person's taste likes a sweeter brandy and one person's might demand a full and pungent brandy. These variations of taste are based on closely guarded blends of the various brandymasters and that's what makes California brandy so exciting. There is a brandy for almost every taste.

The best way to find out what California brandy you like best is to hold a brandy tasting. Gather 8 to 10 friends and have each bring a different brand name of California brandy to your tasting.

Wrap each bottle in aluminum foil so that the label and other signatures are hidden. Follow the professional method of tasting brandy (see above). Make notes on what you like and what you dislike.

Once you have narrowed the field down to one or two brandies, you can proceed to strip the foil off the bottles and see what you and your friends have selected. You will be in for a great surprise.

Let's Explode Some Brandy Myths

Probably one of the greatest myths in the wonderful world of brandy is the snifter myth. This is the myth that says the bigger the snifter, the more you get from the brandy in aroma, taste, bouquet, etc. This is the myth that is displayed in various advertisements in food and wine magazines which show giant snifters of brandy. The truth is that the best snifter is just 6 ounces in size, and it can be cradled between the second and third finger of your hand allowing the palm of your hand to heat the brandy to the proper temperature so that you can enjoy all of the brandy's taste rewards. This is the best way to taste one of nature's great spirits.

Another myth suggests that brandy is strictly a special occasion drink or an after dinner drink. Nonsense! California brandy is much more; it is a spirit that can be drunk before dinner in any number of disguises as well as in after dinner coffees, flips, etc. It is one of the most versatile of drinks.

Let's Cook with Brandy

California brandy is a joyful ingredient in cooking because it contributes a unique flavor to all foods. A simple hamburger sautéed in a skillet can be turned into a gourmet dish in just a few minutes and with few ingredients. After the hamburger is cooked the way you like it, remove it to a warm oven. Pour off half the fat in the pan. Return the skillet to high heat and add ¼ cup California brandy. Heat the brandy to the sizzle, ignite and shake the pan back and forth until the flame dies. Add ½ cup beef stock and reduce by half. Add ¼ cup sour cream and reduce by half. Strain over the hamburgers and serve. What could be more simple to prepare and more delicious to eat.

I don't know why more people do not serve dishes that can be flamed at the table. A simple flaming coffee dish, such as Café Brulot, especially with house lights dimmed, adds a glitter to dining that is unmatched. The "oh's" and "ah's" alone are worth the effort.

Flaming dishes are easy if you know the secret techniques. Always heat the brandy until it sizzles. This means when the tiny bubbles rise from the bottom of the pan to the top, the brandy is at the sizzle. This also means that the alcohol has vaporized and the fumes are ready to be ignited. Stand back and light the rising fumes. Now you can pour the flaming brandy into the dish to be served. Another method is to pour the brandy into the dish with the various ingredients. Heat the dish very hot, ignite the brandy and shake the pan back and forth. When the flame dies out, serve.

Brandy adds flair, zest and style to your cooking. It is easily mastered with a minimum of effort. To get you started, here is a handy guide to gauge the amount of spirit to be added to various dishes.

Dishes

Soups, chowders	½ to 1 cup brandy per 2 quarts of liquid
Stews, ragouts	¼ to ⅓ cup brandy per 1 quart of liquid
Marinades, basting sauces	¼ cup brandy per 1 cup liquid
Flaming meat, poultry, seafood	¼ to ½ cup brandy heated and carefully ignited
Sauces for meats/ pasta/seafood	1 to 2 tablespoons brandy per 1 cup of liquid

Salad dressings	1 tablespoon brandy per 1 cup of liquid
Flambeed fruit	¼ cup brandy heated and carefully ignited
Dessert sauces	1 to 2 tablespoons brandy per 1 cup of liquid
Puddings	2 to 3 tablespoons brandy per 1 package instant pudding mix

Brandied Fruits

Brandied dried apricots	Bring dried apricots to a boil in water, place in a jar, cover with brandy, seal; let stand several weeks.
Brandied cherries	Combine 1 lb. Bing cherries with ½ cup currant jelly, ¼ cup brandy. Refrigerate several hours.
Brandied peaches	Combine ½ cup brandy with 1 package (12 oz.) frozen sliced peaches in syrup. Chill several hours or overnight.
Brandied prunes	Soak desired amount in enough brandy to cover for several hours or overnight. Stuff with blue cheese, or almonds, or snip into small pieces.
Brandied raisins	Combine 1 cup raisins with ½ cup heated brandy in a jar with a tight fitting lid. Let stand 24 hours shaking occasionally.

Common Sense Thinking about Drinking Brandy

In most of the wine producing countries of the world, brandy is the preferred spirit. The reason is simple: brandy comes from wine.

The best way to enjoy brandy is the way you like it. There are no special sacred rules or rituals necessary to the enjoyment of brandy. However, there are some things that you ought to bear in mind.

Snifters—I mentioned it above and I'll say it again: The big fat balloon snifter is total nonsense. The best snifter for pure brandy enjoyment is the 6 ounce model that fits perfectly in your hand and allows you to experience all the brandymaster's skill.

Torching—They still do it in some of the finest restaurants in the United States, and for the life of me I cannot understand how they can destroy in seconds what took years to create. Applying direct flame to a glass of brandy scorches the brandy and severely harshens the flavor. If the waiter pulls this pyromaniac stunt on you, let him drink it and you order a brandy the regular way.

Palming—Somewhere, somebody got the idea that the right way to judge the bouquet of brandy is to put a few drops of the spirit into the palm of your hand and vigorously rub the spirit to warm it. Then raise the palm of your hand to your nose and inhale deeply. More nonsense. The bare palm of anybody's hand has never been known to bring out the bouquet under any circumstances.

Ageing—Unlike wine, brandy ages only when in wood. A brandy that is three years old when bottled will still be three years old even if it is discovered in your grandfather's wine cellar 100 years from now. But the bottle might have some value, since it would be classified as an antique.

Mixing—Purists aside, California brandy is

an excellent mixer. Just read the many recipes herein.

As the subtitle of this book suggests, California brandy is so versatile, that it can be the only liquor you need to entertain. You will find, however, that many of the recipes in this book call for popular liqueurs and other liquors. I recommend adding a selection of them to your bar, for character and versatility to your drink mixing. Purchased in small quantities, they can be added at a minimal cost.

California brandy is an excellent, versatile substitute for many traditional spirits in cocktails. Experiment with your favorite and substitute California brandy for the traditional liquor. I'm sure you'll be surprised. Many say they find a cocktail made from brandy to be milder and more flavorful. I think this is so, because brandy comes from the grape and the grape taste of brandy blends nicely with fruit flavors so popular in cocktails today.

Beverage Service

The well appointed home bar will need a set of glassware to match its entertainment record. If a household entertains up to 12 guests at dinner, the glassware should be as follows:

> 12-8 ounce old fashioned or on-the-rocks glasses
>
> 12-4 to 4½ ounce cocktail glasses
>
> 12-10 ounce highball glasses
>
> 12-8 ounce tulip shaped champagne glasses
>
> 12-9 ounce all purpose wine glasses
>
> 12-6 ounce sherry or dessert wine glasses
>
> 12-6 ounce brandy snifters

It is difficult to ascertain just what supplies will be needed because this must be governed by individual tastes and by the kinds of drinks the host wishes to serve his guests.

Here are two guides to get you started. The first deals with useful bar equipment and the second with useful supplies.

Bar Equipment

Electric blender	Ice bucket
Lemon/lime squeezer	Cocktail shaker
Sharp stainless steel knife	Muddler
Mixing glass	Flat bar strainer
Corkscrew, bottle opener, beer can opener	Long mixing spoons (iced tea spoons will do)
Cocktail, highball glasses	Jigger or measuring cup

Supplies for the Home Bar

Lemons	Limes
Oranges	Maraschino cherries
Small cocktail onions	Small cocktail olives
Sugar, granulated and powdered	Fresh mint
Club soda	Mineral water
Ginger ale	Quinine water/tonic
Bitter lemon	Cola
Grenadine	Orange bitters
Angostura bitters	Dry vermouth
Sweet vermouth	Medium sherry
Tawny port	Vodka
Dry gin	Tequila
Light rum	Dark rum
Bourbon whisky	Scotch whisky
Benedictine	Creme de cacao
Crème de menthe	Coffee liqueur
Tia Maria	Triple sec
California brandy	Orange Curaçao

The home bartender, be it head of the

household or a friend, need abide by only a few rules. Outside of being pleasant, the home bartender ought to remember the following:

• Don't make up more cocktails than are needed to fill the exact number of glasses.

• Cocktails taste better when freshly made.

• Don't allow cocktails to stand. Some of the ingredients will separate. This is true for mixed drinks that contain fruit juices and sugar.

• Cocktails made of liquor and wine can be prepared in advance, but those which call for fruit juices should be mixed just before serving.

• Always inquire about the makeup of the drink ordered. If a friend asks for a dry martini, ask him how dry: 2 to 1, 4 to 1, or 20 to 1. There is a difference.

Measurements used by professional bartenders are in ounces. If you do not have ounce measuring equipment, here's the way to convert to household usage of teaspoons and tablespoons.

¼ ounce	= ½ tablespoon
½ ounce	= 1 tablespoon
¾ ounce	= 1½ tablespoons
1 ounce	= 2 tablespoons
1½ ounces	= 3 tablespoons
1¾ ounces	= 3½ tablespoons
2 ounces	= 4 tablespoons or ¼ cup
1 quart	= 4 cups
1 pint	= 2 cups
½ pint	= 1 cup

Drink Measurements

Drink measurements vary greatly from guide to guide. This book uses the bar jigger (1½ ounces) as a standard measurement. Here's how to convert a jigger to ounces:

½ tablespoon	= ¼ ounce
⅓ jigger or 1 tablespoon	= ½ ounce
½ jigger	= ¾ ounce
⅔ jigger	= 1 ounce
1 jigger	= 1½ ounce
1⅓ jigger	= 2 ounces

Editor's Note: In researching this book, The California Brandy Advisory Board and I were able to uncover more than 800 brandy drink recipes. About half that many are in this guide, because of size limitations. You may, however, request a free list of all titles or of select drink recipes, by sending a self-addressed and stamped #10 envelope to: Brandy Drink Receipes, California Brandy Advisory Board, 426 Pacific Ave., San Francisco, CA 94133.

Finally

Enjoy!!

Cocktails

The cocktail is a purely American institution and undoubtedly America's most noted contribution to the wonderful world of bibulous pleasure. However, the origin of the name "cocktail" is a curious mixture of fact, fiction and folklore. Here are a few such stories to think about as you sip your favorite cocktail.

*Southern army officers were once served a luscious mixed drink by a stunning Southern belle. Her name? Octelle, sir.

*Western horse traders whose horses weren't worth their pelts, often gave their horses liquor which made them lively as well as made them cock their tails.

*According to James Fenimore Cooper, an Irish lass named Betsy Flanagan not only got chickens from her Tory farmers but decorated the French and American soldier's drinks with the feathers from the cock's tail.

Whether or not any of these stories are true, the cocktail is truly American. And today, we Americans are the foremost masters of the cocktail. If you don't think so, we invite you to sample the hundreds of cocktails listed herein.

ADAM & EVE

⅔ jigger Forbidden Fruit
⅔ jigger gin
⅔ jigger California brandy
1 dash lemon juice

Shake well with ice and strain into a cocktail glass. Makes 1 drink.

ADIOS AMIGOS

⅔ jigger light rum
⅓ jigger dry vermouth
⅓ jigger California brandy
⅓ jigger gin
½ jigger lime juice

Shake well with ice and strain into a cocktail glass. Makes 1 drink.

ALEXANDER'S SISTER

¾ jigger California brandy
¾ jigger crème de menthe
¾ jigger heavy cream

Shake well with ice. Strain into a chilled cocktail glass. Makes 1 drink.

BRANDIED MADEIRA

⅔ jigger Madeira wine
⅔ jigger California brandy
⅓ jigger dry vermouth
Lemon twist

Stir well with ice and strain into a cocktail glass. Add lemon twist. Makes 1 drink.

ANGEL'S KISS

¼ dark crème de cacao
¼ creme d'Yvette
¼ California brandy
¼ cream

Into a cordial glass pour one ingredient at a time in order listed over spoon, to form layers. Be careful they do not mix. Makes 1 drink.

APOLLO MOON MAIDEN

⅔ jigger Galliano
⅔ jigger California brandy
1 jigger cream
3 drops vanilla extract
Lime slice

Shake well with ice and strain into a cocktail glass. Makes 1 drink.

APPLE BRANDY DAISY

1 jigger apple brandy
⅔ jigger California brandy
1 jigger lemon juice
1 teaspoon sugar
⅓ jigger grenadine
Lemon wedge
Cherry

Shake with ice and strain into a large cocktail glass. Add fruit garnish. Makes 1 drink.

To keep California brandy strictly a California product, the brandy is aged exclusively in American oak barrels, specially chosen for their unique properties.

B & B

⅔ jigger Benedictine
⅔ jigger California brandy

Pour Benedictine into bottom of a liqueur glass. Gently pour brandy on top. Makes 1 drink.

BALTIMORE BRACER

1 jigger California brandy
1 jigger anisette
1 egg white

Shake with ice and strain into a cocktail glass. Makes 1 drink.

BAYOU

1 jigger California brandy
½ tablespoon peach brandy
⅓ jigger mango nectar
½ tablespoon lime juice
Peach slice

Shake well with ice and strain into a cocktail glass. Garnish with a peach slice. Makes 1 drink.

BEN BRANDY

1 jigger California brandy
⅓ jigger Benedictine
⅓ jigger orange juice
Red cherry

Fill old-fashioned glass with ice cubes. Add ingredients and garnish with cherry. Makes 1 drink.

BETSY ROSS

1 jigger California brandy
1 jigger port wine
1 dash angostura bitters
1 dash orange curaçao
Orange peel

Stir well with ice and strain into a wine glass.
Garnish with orange peel. Makes 1 drink.

BETTER THAN ANYTHING

2 jiggers California brandy
⅓ jigger grenadine
⅓ jigger orange curaçao
2 jiggers cherry brandy
⅓ jigger lemon juice

Shake with cracked ice and strain into a cocktail glass. Makes 1 drink.

BETWEEN THE SHEETS

½ jigger California brandy
½ jigger light rum
½ jigger Cointreau or triple sec
⅓ jigger lemon juice
Lemon wedge

Shake well with ice and strain into a chilled
cocktail glass. Garnish with lemon wedge.
Makes 1 drink.

*Early French soldiers carried two flasks with
them into battle. One contained gun powder and
the other contained brandy. Thankfully, they
never got the two mixed up.*

BLACK PEARL

½ jigger Tia Maria
½ jigger California brandy
Champagne
Black cherry

Pour Tia Maria and brandy into a cocktail or champagne glass. Fill with champagne and garnish with a cherry. Makes 1 drink.

BOB DANBY

1 jigger Dubonnet
½ jigger California brandy

Stir well with ice and strain into a cocktail glass. Makes 1 drink.

BRANANA

⅔ jigger California brandy
⅔ jigger crème de banana
⅔ jigger sweet-and-sour mix

Blend with crushed ice and pour into sour glass. Makes 1 drink.

BRANDIED APRICOT FLIP

1 egg
1 teaspoon sugar
1 jigger California brandy
⅓ jigger apricot brandy
Nutmeg

Shake with ice and strain into a sour or cocktail glass. Dust with nutmeg. Makes 1 drink.

BRANDY ALEXANDER

¾ jigger California brandy
¾ jigger crème de cacao
¾ jigger heavy cream

Shake well with ice and strain into a chilled cocktail glass. Makes 1 drink.

BRANDYAMER

1⅓ jiggers California brandy
⅓ jigger Amer Picon
Lemon twist
Orange peel

Stir with ice and strain into a cocktail glass. Add lemon and orange garnishes. Makes 1 drink.

BRANDY AND SODA

Place ice cubes in an old-fashioned glass and add ⅔ jigger California brandy. Fill with soda.

BRANDY BLUSH

1⅓ jiggers California brandy
⅓ jigger maraschino cherry juice
2 dashes bitters
Lemon wedge
Soda water, chilled
2 maraschino cherries

Over ice cubes in double old-fashioned glass, pour brandy, cherry juice and bitters. Squeeze in juice of lemon and add rind. Add soda water to taste, then stir once. Garnish with 2 maraschino cherries. Makes 1 drink.

BRANDY CASSIS

¾ jigger California brandy
⅓ jigger fresh lemon juice
½ tablespoon crème de cassis
Lemon twist

Combine California brandy and lemon juice in old-fashioned glass. Float crème de cassis on top. Garnish with lemon twist. Makes 1 drink.

BRANDY CHAPALA

1 jigger tequila
⅓ jigger lemon juice
½ jigger California brandy
1 teaspoon grenadine
Lemon slice

Shake well with ice and strain over ice cubes into an old-fashioned glass. Garnish with lemon slice. Makes 1 drink.

BRANDY COCKTAIL

2 jiggers California brandy
½ jigger orange curaçao
1 dash angostura bitters
Lemon twist

Stir well with ice and strain into a cocktail glass. Serve with a lemon twist. Makes 1 drink. Another version features Cointreau instead of curaçao.

The brandy capital consuming of the United States is Milwaukee, Wisconsin. Where is the brandymaking capital of the United States? Would you believe Fresno!

BRANDY CRUSTA

Orange juice
Granulated sugar
1 (6-inch) long lemon peel
1⅓ jiggers California brandy
⅓ jigger Cointreau
⅔ jigger lemon juice
⅓ jigger simple syrup
1 dash grenadine
¾ cup bar ice

Wet rim of 6-ounce glass with orange juice and dip in sugar. Twist lemon peel into glass. Combine remaining ingredients in blender, pour over peel and serve. Makes 1 drink.

BRANDY FLIP

1 jigger California brandy
1 teaspoon superfine sugar
1 egg
2 teaspoons heavy cream (optional)
Nutmeg

Shake all ingredients except nutmeg vigorously with ice and strain into a cocktail glass. Lightly sprinkle nutmeg over top. Makes 1 drink.

BRANDY FLOAT

1 jigger California brandy
Soda water

Place several ice cubes in an old-fashioned glass and fill with soda water. Float brandy by carefully pouring it over the bowl of a teaspoon so that it flows on the surface but does not mix. Makes 1 drink.

BRANDY GRASSHOPPER

⅔ **jigger California brandy**
⅔ **jigger green crème de menthe**
⅔ **jigger white crème de cacao**
1⅓ **jiggers light cream**
½ **cup crushed ice**
Mint sprig (optional)

Whirl all ingredients in blender and serve in an 8-ounce stemmed champagne glass. Garnish with mint sprig, if desired. This drink may also be served "on the rocks." Makes 1 drink.

BRANDY MANHATTAN

1⅓ **jiggers California brandy**
⅓ **jigger sweet vermouth**
1 **dash bitters (optional)**
Maraschino cherry
Lemon peel

Mix brandy, vermouth and bitters well with ice and strain into chilled cocktail glass. Add cherry and twist lemon peel. For a dry brandy manhattan, use dry vermouth instead of sweet. For variety, use half dry and half sweet vermouth. Makes 1 drink.

BRANDY MELBA

1 **jigger California brandy**
½ **tablespoon peach brandy**
½ **tablespoon grenadine**
1 **tablespoon lemon juice**
1 **dash orange bitters**

Shake well with ice and strain into a cocktail glass. Makes 1 drink.

BRANDY OLD-FASHIONED

½ teaspoon sugar
2 dashes angostura bitters
1 jigger California brandy
Orange slice
Maraschino cherry

Place sugar, dissolved in a little water or soda water, and bitters in an old-fashioned glass and fill with ice. Add brandy and garnish with fruit. Makes 1 drink.

BRANDY SANGAREE

½ teaspoon sugar
1 jigger California brandy
Nutmeg

In a small tumbler, place sugar dissolved in a little water. Add brandy and ice. Stir, then dust with nutmeg. Makes 1 drink.

BRANDY SOUR

Juice of ½ lemon
½ tablespoon sugar
⅔ jigger California brandy
Soda water
Orange slice
Cherry

Shake lemon, sugar and brandy and strain into medium glass. Add a squirt of soda water and garnish with fruit. Makes 1 drink.

George Washington was a brandy fancier. More than 150 gallons of various brandies were discovered in his cellars at Mr. Vernon.

BRANDY STOUT

1 jigger California brandy
Stout

Pour brandy into 6-ounce wine glass and swirl to coat sides. Fill with stout. Makes 1 drink.

BRANDY VERMOUTH

3 jiggers California brandy
1 jigger sweet vermouth
1 dash angostura bitters

Stir with ice and strain into a cocktail glass. Makes 1 drink.

BRANTINI
(Brandy Martini)

1 jigger California brandy
⅔ jigger gin
½ tablespoon dry vermouth
Lemon twist
Olive

Stir well with ice and strain into a cocktail glass. Decorate with lemon twist and olive. Makes 1 drink.

BROWN DERBY

½ jigger California brandy
½ jigger Vandermint
1½ tablespoons heavy cream

Combine ingredients over ice cubes in an old-fashioned glass. Makes 1 drink.

CALCUTTA

1 jigger California brandy
1 jigger dry vermouth
1 jigger sweet white vermouth
1 teaspoon Cointreau
1 teaspoon green Chartreuse

Stir well with ice and strain into chilled cocktail glass. Makes 1 drink.

CALIFORNIA CABLE CAR

⅔ jigger lime juice
½ jigger California brandy
½ jigger rum
½ jigger triple sec

Shake well with ice and strain into a cocktail glass. Makes 1 drink.

CALIFORNIA CONNECTION

⅔ jigger California brandy
⅔ jigger port
½ tablespoon Pernod
½ tablespoon lemon juice
2 dashes Peychaud's bitters

Stir well with ice and strain into a cocktail glass. Makes 1 drink.

PEACOCK

1 jigger California brandy
⅓ jigger Amer Picon
⅓ jigger Pernod

Shake well with ice and strain into a cocktail glass. Makes 1 drink.

CALIFORNIA DRIVER
(Brandy Screwdriver)

1 jigger California brandy
½ cup cold orange juice
1 teaspoon lemon juice (optional)

Shake well with ice or blend at high speed for 5 seconds. Strain into chilled glass. Makes 1 drink.

CALIFORNIA SWISS ALEXANDER

⅔ jigger cream
½ jigger Cheri Suisse
½ jigger California brandy

Shake well with ice and strain into a cocktail glass. Makes 1 drink.

CALIXICO

2 jiggers California brandy
½ jigger Kahlua

Combine in an old-fashioned glass filled with crushed ice. Makes 1 drink.

CECIL PICK-ME-UP

2 jiggers California brandy
1 teaspoon sugar
1 egg yolk
Champagne, iced

Shake brandy, sugar and yolk well with ice and strain into a large cocktail glass. Fill with champagne. Makes 1 drink.

CEMENT BOOT

⅕ crème de cassis
⅕ light crème de cacao
⅕ green crème de menthe
⅕ Tia Maria
⅕ California brandy

Into a cordial glass place one ingredient at a time in order listed to form layers. Be careful they do not mix. Makes 1 drink.

CHAMPS ELYSEES

1 jigger California brandy
½ jigger green Chartreuse
⅓ jigger Rose's lime juice
1 dash orange bitters

Shake well with ice and strain over ice cubes in a chilled old-fashioned glass. Makes 1 drink.

CLARET COCKTAIL

⅔ jigger dry red wine
⅔ jigger California brandy
½ tablespoon orange curaçao
½ tablespoon lemon juice
1 dash anisette
Orange peel

Stir with ice and strain into a cocktail glass. Makes 1 drink.

One day President Lincoln received some complaints about General Grant's drinking. Lincoln suggested that they find out what Grant was drinking so he could send a barrel to each of his generals. Grant's drink of course was brandy.

CLUB

1 jigger California brandy
1 dash orange bitters
½ tablespoon maraschino liqueur
½ tablespoon pineapple syrup

Stir well with ice and strain into a cocktail glass. Makes 1 drink.

COFFEE ALEXANDER

⅔ jigger California brandy
⅔ jigger coffee liqueur
⅔ jigger cream

Shake well with ice and strain into a cocktail glass. Makes 1 drink.

COOL BRANDY

1 jigger California brandy
⅓ jigger white crème de menthe
⅓ jigger lime juice

Shake all ingredients vigorously with ice until well chilled. Strain into a cocktail glass or over ice cubes in an old-fashioned glass. Makes 1 drink.

CORONATION

2 jiggers California brandy
1 jigger curaçao
1 dash peach bitters
1 dash white crème de menthe or peppermint

Stir with ice and strain into a cocktail glass. Makes 1 drink.

CORPSE REVIVER

⅓ jigger sweet vermouth
⅓ jigger apple brandy
⅔ jigger California brandy

Shake well with ice and strain into a cocktail glass. Makes 1 drink.

COSSACK

½ jigger sugar syrup
1 jigger lime juice
2 jiggers vodka
2 jiggers California brandy

Shake with crushed ice and pour into a cocktail glass. Makes 1 drink.

CREAMY ORANGE

⅔ jigger orange juice
⅔ jigger cream sherry
⅓ jigger cream
½ tablespoon California brandy

Shake well with ice and strain into a cocktail glass. Makes 1 drink.

CUBAN

Juice of ½ lime or ¼ lemon
⅓ jigger apricot brandy
⅔ jigger California brandy

Shake well with ice and strain into a cocktail glass. Makes 1 drink.

DELMONICO

⅔ jigger gin
⅓ jigger dry vermouth
⅓ jigger sweet vermouth
⅓ jigger California brandy
1 dash angostura bitters
Orange peel

Stir with ice and strain into a cocktail glass.
Add orange garnish. Makes 1 drink.

DEPTH BOMB

1 jigger apple brandy
1 jigger California brandy
¼ teaspoon grenadine
¼ teaspoon lemon juice

Shake with ice and strain into a cocktail glass.
Makes 1 drink. The Depth Bomb is also
known as the "Depth Charge." Whatever the
name, it has a reputation for going off when
it hits bottom.

DUTCH ALEXANDER

⅔ jigger California brandy
⅔ jigger cream
⅔ jigger Vandermint

Shake well with ice and strain into a cocktail
glass. Makes 1 drink.

EASY MONEY

⅔ jigger scotch
⅔ jigger California brandy

Combine in an old-fashioned glass and fill
with ice. Makes 1 drink.

FANCY FRIEND

⅔ jigger California brandy
1 dash bitters
Champagne, iced

Into a sugar-rimmed cocktail glass pour
brandy and bitters. Fill with champagne.
Makes 1 drink.

FAVORITE

1 jigger port
½ jigger California brandy

Stir with ice and strain into a cocktail glass.
Makes 1 drink.

FIREWORKS

½ tablespoon grenadine
½ tablespoon crème de cassis
½ tablespoon melon-flavored liqueur
½ tablespoon apricot brandy
½ tablespoon Cointreau
½ tablespoon California brandy

Using a straight sided narrow 2-ounce glass,
float one liqueur on another in order of ingredients listed to form layers. Be careful they
don't mix. Makes 1 drink.

*If the Hollywood scriptwriters had done their
homework, you wouldn't have heard John
Wayne or Gary Cooper mosey up to the bar and
say, "Whisky." They would have said "Brandy,
bartender," because brandy was the beverage
preferred by the men who settled the West.*

FLORIDA PUNCH

⅔ **jigger grapefruit juice**
⅔ **jigger orange juice**
⅔ **jigger dark rum**
⅓ **jigger California brandy**

Shake well with ice and strain into a cocktail glass. Makes 1 drink.

FOREIGN AID

1 **jigger California brandy**
½ **jigger amaretto**

Pour ingredients over ice into an old-fashioned glass. Makes 1 drink. Also known as: Beautiful & French Connection.

BRANDY FINO

1 **jigger California brandy**
⅓ **jigger dry sherry**
⅓ **jigger Drambuie**
Lemon twist
Orange peel

Stir ingredients with ice and strain into a cocktail glass. Add lemon and orange garnishes. Makes 1 drink.

CHAMPAGNE POLONAISE

⅔ **jigger blackberry brandy**
½ **tablespoon California brandy**
Champagne, iced

Pour brandies into champagne glass. Fill with champagne. Makes 1 drink.

FOXHOUND

1 jigger California brandy
1 jigger cranberry juice
½ tablespoon Kümmel
½ tablespoon lemon juice

Shake well with ice and strain into a cocktail glass. Makes 1 drink.

GEORGIA

1 jigger California brandy
⅓ jigger Grand Marnier

Combine ingredients in an old-fashioned glass or snifter. Makes 1 drink.

GIN BLIND

1 jigger gin
⅓ jigger orange curaçao
½ tablespoon California brandy
1 dash orange bitters

Stir well with ice and strain into cocktail glass. Makes 1 drink.

GLOOM LIFTER

⅔ jigger lemon juice
½ teaspoon sugar
½ egg white
⅓ jigger grenadine
1 jigger Irish whisky
½ tablespoon California brandy

Shake well with ice and strain into a cocktail glass. Makes 1 drink.

GOOD LIFE

1 jigger California brandy
⅓ jigger orange curaçao

Pour ingredients into an old-fashioned glass.
Fill with ice. Makes 1 drink.

GRAND SLAM

⅓ jigger gin
⅓ jigger California brandy
½ jigger apricot brandy
⅓ jigger lime juice

Shake well with ice and strain into a cocktail
glass. Makes 1 drink.

GREEN DRAGON

1 jigger green Chartreuse
1 jigger California brandy

Stir with shaved ice and strain into a cocktail
glass. Makes 1 drink.

GREEN HORNET

½ jigger California brandy
½ jigger melon-flavored liqueur

Pour over ice and strain into a martini glass.
Makes 1 drink.

HARMONY

⅓ jigger strawberry syrup
⅓ jigger maraschino syrup
⅔ jigger lemon juice
2⅔ jiggers California brandy

Shake well with cracked ice and serve in
cocktail glasses. Makes 2 drinks.

HARVARD

1 jigger California brandy
½ jigger dry white vermouth
1 teaspoon grenadine
1 teaspoon lemon juice

Shake well with ice and strain into a cocktail
glass. Makes 1 drink.

HAWAIIAN CONNECTION

¾ jigger California brandy
½ tablespoon Hawaiian coffee liqueur

Combine brandy and coffee liqueur in brandy
snifter. Makes 1 drink.

H-BOMB

⅓ jigger yellow Chartreuse
⅓ jigger green Chartreuse
½ jigger California brandy
½ jigger bourbon

Shake well with ice and strain into a cocktail
glass. Makes 1 drink.

HEALTH COCKTAIL

1 jigger California brandy
⅔ cup Hercules

Stir slightly with ice and strain into a cocktail glass. Makes 1 drink.

HELL'S BELLS

1 jigger California brandy
⅓ jigger green crème de menthe
Red pepper

Pour brandy and crème de menthe in an old-fashioned glass, then sprinkle red pepper over top. Makes 1 drink.

HIGH HAT

¾ jigger California brandy
¾ jigger grapefruit juice
Sugar to taste

Shake well with ice and strain into a cocktail glass. Makes 1 drink.

HOP FROG

⅔ jigger California brandy
1 jigger lime juice
Sweetener to taste

Shake brandy, lime juice and desired sweetener (sugar, honey, etc.) with ice and strain into a cocktail glass. Makes 1 drink.

IRISH STINGER

½ jigger Irish whisky
½ jigger California brandy
½ jigger green crème de menthe

Shake well with ice and strain into a chilled cocktail glass. Makes 1 drink.

ITALIAN STINGER

1 jigger California brandy
1 jigger Galliano

Shake well with ice and strain into a cocktail glass. Makes 1 drink.

JERSEY

⅓ jigger green Chartreuse
⅓ jigger California brandy

Into a cordial glass carefully pour Chartreuse, then brandy so that the two do not mix. Makes 1 drink.

JOHN ADAMS

John Adams, Thomas Jefferson and George Washington each favored brandy in their drinks and cooking.

1 jigger California brandy
1 jigger apple brandy
1 dash orange bitters
Orange twist

Shake well with ice and strain into a chilled cocktail glass. Garnish with an orange twist. Makes 1 drink.

KING'S PEG

1 jigger California brandy
Champagne, iced

Add brandy to large wine glass with 1 ice
cube in it. Fill with champagne. Makes 1
drink.

KISS THE BOYS GOODBYE

1⅓ jiggers lemon juice
1 jigger sloe gin
1 jigger California brandy
1 whole egg white

Shake well with ice and strain into a cocktail
glass. Makes 2 drinks.

KNIGHT

1 jigger California brandy
1 jigger lemon juice
½ tablespoon Cointreau
½ tablespoon yellow Chartreuse

Shake well with ice and strain into a cocktail
glass. Makes 1 drink.

LADY BE GOOD

1 jigger California brandy
½ jigger white crème de menthe
½ jigger sweet vermouth

Shake with cracked ice and strain into a cocktail glass. Makes 1 drink.

LA JOLLA

1 jigger California brandy
⅓ jigger crème de banana
½ tablespoon lemon juice
½ tablespoon orange juice

Shake well with ice and strain into a sugar-rimmed cocktail glass. Makes 1 drink.

LEMON BRANDY

1 jigger California brandy
⅓ jigger lemon juice

Shake well with ice and strain into a cocktail glass. Makes 1 drink.

LOVER'S DELIGHT

½ jigger Cointreau
½ jigger forbidden fruit
⅔ jigger California brandy

Shake with ice and strain into a cocktail glass. Makes 1 drink.

MAE WEST

1 jigger California brandy
1 egg yolk
1 teaspoon sugar
Cayenne pepper

Shake well with ice and strain into a sour glass. Sprinkle cayenne pepper over top. Makes 1 drink.

MAPLE BRANDY

1 jigger California brandy
⅔ jigger lemon juice
1 teaspoon maple syrup
Orange slice
Maraschino cherry

Shake brandy, lemon juice and maple syrup
vigorously with ice and strain into a cocktail
glass. Add fruit garnishes. Makes 1 drink.

MAY FLOWER

1 jigger Red Dubonnet
½ jigger California brandy

Stir well with ice and strain into a cocktail
glass. Makes 1 drink.

McBRANDY

1 jigger California brandy
½ jigger apple juice
½ tablespoon lemon juice
Lemon slice

Shake well with ice and strain into a cocktail
glass. Add a lemon garnish. Makes 1 drink.

DEVIL

½ jigger California brandy
½ jigger green creme de menthe
Red pepper

Shake brandy and creme de menthe with ice
and strain into a cocktail glass. Sprinkle red
pepper over top. Makes 1 drink.

MEXICAN GRASSHOPPER

⅔ jigger California brandy
⅔ jigger green crème de menthe
⅔ jigger Kahlua
1⅓ jiggers light cream
½ cup crushed ice
Mint sprig (optional)

Whirl ingredients in blender and serve in 8-ounce stemmed champagne glass. Garnish with mint sprig, if desired. May also be served "on the rocks." Makes 1 drink.

MONTAUK RIDING CLUB

⅔ jigger Calisay
¾ jigger California brandy
½ tablespoon lime juice
¼ teaspoon sugar

Shake well with ice and strain into a cocktail glass. Makes 1 drink.

MORNING TOUCH

2 dashes curaçao
2 dashes maraschino liqueur
2 dashes orange bitters
2 dashes Pernod
⅔ jigger California brandy
⅔ jigger dry vermouth
Maraschino cherry
Lemon peel

Shake well with ice and strain into a cocktail glass. Add a cherry and squeeze lemon peel over top. Makes 1 drink.

MUSCATEL FLIP

1 jigger Muscatel wine
½ jigger California brandy
1 egg
1 teaspoon sugar
⅓ jigger cream
Nutmeg

Shake well with ice and strain into a sour glass. Top with nutmeg sprinkle. Makes 1 drink.

NONE BUT THE BRAVE

2 jiggers California brandy
1 jigger pimento dram
1 teaspoon powdered sugar
1 dash Jamaica ginger
1 dash lemon juice

Shake with ice and strain into a cocktail glass. Makes 1 drink.

ORANGE CUP

⅓ jigger California brandy
⅔ jigger orange juice
⅔ jigger cream sherry
⅓ jigger Cointreau
⅔ jigger heavy cream

Blend with crushed ice and strain into a wine glass. Makes 1 drink.

PEPPERMINT STICK

1 jigger California brandy
⅓ jigger orange curaçao
⅓ jigger peppermint schnapps
1 dash orange or peach bitters

Shake well with ice and strain into a cocktail glass. Makes 1 drink.

PHEOBE SNOW

⅔ jigger California brandy
⅔ jigger Dubonnet
4 dashes Pernod

Shake well with ice and strain into a cocktail glass. Makes 1 drink.

PICKFAIR

1 jigger California brandy
⅓ jigger cola
⅓ jigger lemon syrup

Shake well with ice and strain into a cocktail glass. Makes 1 drink.

POLYNESIAN APPLE

¾ jigger apple brandy
⅓ jigger California brandy
½ jigger pineapple juice
Pineapple spear

Shake brandies and juice well with ice and strain into a cocktail glass. Add pineapple garnish. Makes 1 drink.

POUSSE CAFE

⅓ jigger grenadine
⅓ jigger maraschino liqueur
⅓ jigger green crème de menthe
⅓ jigger crème de violette
⅓ jigger Chartreuse
⅓ jigger California brandy

Pour the above in the order listed into a cordial glass. Be careful they do not mix. Makes 1 drink.

PRAIRIE OYSTER

1 jigger California brandy
1 egg
1 dash Worcestershire sauce
Salt (optional)

Carefully break egg into a 6-ounce glass. Add Worcestershire sauce and brandy. Blend lightly with egg white, keeping yolk intact. Makes 1 drink.

PRINCE CHARLIE

½ jigger Drambuie
½ jigger California brandy
½ jigger lemon juice

Shake with cracked ice and strain into a cocktail glass. Makes 1 drink.

One of the best drinks in the world is the least complicated: a few ounces of California brandy over ice.

QUEEN ELIZABETH

¾ jigger California brandy
⅔ jigger sweet vermouth
½ tablespoon orange curaçao
Maraschino cherry (optional)

Stir well with ice and strain into a cocktail
glass. Garnish with cherry if desired. Makes 1
drink.

QUICKLY

⅔ jigger California brandy
⅔ jigger anisette
⅓ jigger orange curaçao
2 dashes angostura bitters

Shake well with ice and strain into a cocktail
glass. Makes 1 drink.

QUINQUINA

½ jigger California brandy
½ jigger peach brandy
½ jigger Quinquina
½ jigger Pernod

Shake well with ice and strain into a cocktail
glass. Makes 1 drink.

*Unlike wine, brandy does not age in the bottle.
The law states that California brandy must
be aged two years in wood, but most brandy
distillers age their spirits twice that long to
achieve a depth of flavor and a special
mellowness.*

RAINBOW

¹/₇ yellow Chartreuse
¹/₇ green Chartreuse
¹/₇ crème de cacao
¹/₇ crème de violette
¹/₇ maraschino liqueur
¹/₇ Benedictine
¹/₇ California brandy

Into a large cordial glass pour one ingredient at a time in order listed to form layers. Be careful they don't mix. Makes 1 drink.

RAJAH

¾ jigger California brandy
¾ jigger champagne

Stir with ice and strain into a cocktail glass. Makes 1 drink.

RENDEZVOUS

²/₃ jigger California brandy
½ jigger Strega
½ jigger cherry brandy
Pineapple slice

Shake well with ice and strain into a cocktail glass. Garnish with pineapple. Makes 1 drink.

RUBY

⅓ jigger Galliano
²/₃ jigger California brandy
⅓ jigger cherry kijafa
⅓ jigger orange juice

Shake well with ice and strain into a cocktail glass. Makes 1 drink.

RUSSIAN COCKTAIL

1 jigger California brandy
⅓ jigger orange juice
½ tablespoon Pernod
1 dash orange bitters

Shake well with ice and strain into a cocktail glass. Makes 1 drink.

SANTA FE

1 jigger California brandy
⅓ jigger grapefruit juice
⅓ jigger dry vermouth
½ tablespoon lemon juice

Shake well with ice and strain into a sugar-rimmed cocktail glass. Makes 1 drink.

SARONNO

½ jigger amaretto
½ jigger California brandy
⅔ jigger cream

Shake well or blend with ice and strain into a cocktail glass. Makes 1 drink.

SAVOY HOTEL

1 jigger California brandy
1 jigger Benedictine
1 jigger crème de cacao

Into a cordial glass pour ingredients one at a time in order listed to form layers. Be careful they do not mix. Makes 1 drink.

SIDECAR

½ jigger California brandy
½ jigger triple sec, orange curaçao or
  Cointreau
½ jigger lemon juice

Shake well with ice and strain into a chilled cocktail glass. Proportions may be varied to taste. For stronger brandy flavor, use 1 jigger California brandy and ⅓ jigger each of the other two ingredients. Makes 1 drink.

SIR KNIGHT

⅔ jigger California brandy
½ jigger Cointreau
½ jigger yellow Chartreuse
1 dash angostura bitters
Lemon twist

Stir with ice and strain into a cocktail glass. Makes 1 drink.

SIR WALTER ("Swalter")

⅔ cup California brandy
⅓ cup light rum
1 teaspoon grenadine
1 teaspoon orange curaçao
1 teaspoon lemon juice

Shake well with ice and strain into cocktail glasses. Makes 2 drinks.

SLAM

½ jigger California brandy
½ jigger Cointreau
⅓ jigger apricot brandy
⅓ jigger lime juice

Shake well with ice and strain into a cocktail glass. Makes 1 drink.

SLOE BRANDY

1 jgger California brandy
⅓ jigger sloe gin
½ tablespoon lemon juice
Lemon twist

Shake well with ice and strain into a cocktail glass. Makes 1 drink.

SNIFTER

1 jigger Galliano
1 jigger California brandy
½ jigger white crème de menthe

Pour ingredients into brandy snifter. Fill with crushed ice and serve with short straw. Makes 1 drink.

SOUTHERN PACIFIC

1 jigger California brandy
⅓ jigger lemon juice
⅓ jigger crème de banana
½ tablespoon white crème de menthe
Pineapple spear

Shake well with ice and strain into a cocktail glass. Garnish with pineapple. Makes 1 drink.

STINGER

1 jigger white crème de menthe
2 jiggers California brandy
Lemon twist (optional)

Shake well with ice and strain into a cocktail glass. Add lemon twist if desired. Makes 1 drink. For a Stinger Royal, add ⅔ jigger Pernod.

STIRRUP CUP

⅔ jigger lemon juice
½ jigger California brandy
½ jigger cherry brandy

Shake well with ice and strain into a cocktail glass. Makes 1 drink.

STRAWBERRY SHAKE

1 jigger California brandy
2 dashes orange bitters
⅔ jigger strawberry juice (from fresh berries)
Strawberry

Shake well with ice and strain into a cocktail glass. Garnish with a fresh strawberry. Makes 1 drink.

SUN AND SHADE

¾ jigger California brandy
¾ jigger gin

Shake well with ice and strain into a cocktail glass. Makes 1 drink.

SUNDOWNER

⅓ **jigger lemon juice**
⅓ **jigger orange juice**
⅔ **jigger Van der Hum liqueur**
2 **jiggers California brandy**

Shake well with ice and strain into sour glasses. Makes 2 drinks.

SUNSET

2 **jiggers California brandy**
Rind of 1 orange, slivered thin
1 **teaspoon peach preserve**
1 **apricot, sliced, with crushed pit**
3 **jiggers dry gin**
3 **jiggers white wine**
1 **jigger dry vermouth**

Soak brandy, orange rind, peach preserve, apricot and pit for 2 hours. Add gin, wine and vermouth. Shake well with ice and strain into cocktail glasses. Serves 6.

SWORD'S EDGE

1⅓ **jiggers California brandy**
⅓ **jigger sweet vermouth**

Stir well with ice and strain into a cocktail glass. Makes 1 drink.

Americans prefer a lighter brandy. This distinctive lightness of California brandy is primarily a result of the relatively new continuous distillation method used overwhelmingly to allow for precise computer-like control which makes for a more consistent product.

TANTALUS

⅓ jigger lemon juice
⅓ jigger California brandy
⅓ jigger forbidden fruit

Shake well with ice and strain into a cocktail glass. Makes 1 drink.

TEXAS SPECIAL

½ jigger gin
½ jigger grapefruit juice
½ tablespoon California brandy
½ jigger dry vermouth
⅓ jigger Cointreau

Shake well with ice and strain into a cocktail glass. Makes 1 drink.

THUMPER

1 jigger California brandy
½ jigger Tuaca
Lemon twist

Stir well with ice and strain into a cocktail glass. Add lemon twist. Makes 1 drink.

THUNDER AND LIGHTNING

2 jiggers California brandy
1 egg yolk
1 teaspoon powdered sugar or sugar syrup
Cayenne pepper

Shake well with ice and strain into a medium size glass. Sprinkle pepper over top. Makes 1 drink.

TIGER'S MILK

¾ jigger sloe gin
¾ jigger California brandy
Lemon twist

Shake well with ice and strain into a cocktail glass. Add a lemon twist. Makes 1 drink.

TONGUE TWISTER

⅓ jigger port
⅓ jigger California brandy
⅓ jigger apricot brandy
1 egg yolk
1 teaspoon sugar
Lemon twist
Cinnamon

Shake well with ice and strain into a cocktail glass. Add lemon twist and sprinkle with cinnamon. Makes 1 drink.

TROPICAL

1 jigger California brandy
⅓ jigger crème de vanilla
½ tablespoon Pernod

Shake with ice and pour into a cocktail glass. Makes 1 drink.

The greatest gourmet ever to serve as President of the United States was Thomas Jefferson. He enjoyed his food smothered with wine or brandy. His brandied peaches were saturated with a pint of brandy which were served at special dinners and also placed in storage for future use.

TUESDAY WELD

½ jigger California brandy
½ jigger dark crème de cacao
⅔ jigger cream
1 Oreo cookie

Shake well with ice and strain into a cocktail glass. Place Oreo in the glass and serve. Makes 1 drink.

VANDERBILT HOTEL

3 jiggers California brandy
1 jigger cherry brandy
2 dashes angostura bitters
2 dashes sugar syrup

Stir with ice and strain into a cocktail glass. Makes 1 drink.

VIA VENETO CALIFORNIAN

2 jiggers California brandy
⅔ jigger Sambuca
1 egg white
⅔ jigger lemon juice
2 teaspoons sugar

Shake well with ice and strain into cocktail glasses. Makes 2 drinks.

HARRY'S PICK-ME-UP

2 jiggers California brandy
1 teaspoon grenadine
Juice of ½ lemon
Champagne, iced

Shake brandy, grenadine and lemon juice with ice and strain into a cocktail glass. Fill with champagne. Makes 1 drink.

VIRGIN SPECIAL

1 cup red-currant juice
½ cup gooseberry syrup
1 cup fresh raspberries
1 cup California brandy
2 cups gin
1 cup white wine
Raspberry or red-currant garnish

Lightly mash a glassful of fresh raspberries in a bowl. Onto the fruit pour the brandy, gin, currant juice and gooseberry syrup in that order. Let stand 1 hour. Add the wine and ice, then shake well. Pour into individual glasses and garnish with raspberry or small sprig of red currants. Serves 6.

WHICH WAY?

⅓ cup California brandy
⅓ cup Pernod
⅓ cup anisette

Shake well with ice and strain into cocktail glasses. Makes 2 drinks.

WHITE LADY

1 jigger Cointreau
⅓ jigger California brandy
⅓ jigger white crème de menthe

Shake well with ice and strain into a cocktail glass. Makes 1 drink.

WILLIE SMITH

⅔ jigger California brandy
⅓ jigger maraschino liqueur
2 dashes lemon juice

Shake well with ice and strain into a cocktail glass. Makes 1 drink.

WITCH DOCTOR

1 jigger California brandy
¼ cup cream or half-and-half

Shake well with ice and strain into a cocktail glass. Makes 1 drink.

WOW

1⅓ jiggers California brandy
1⅓ jiggers apple brandy
1⅓ jiggers Hercules
1⅓ jiggers rum

Shake well with ice and strain into cocktail glasses. Makes 2 drinks.

YELLOW ROSE

1⅓ jiggers California brandy
⅓ jigger triple sec
2⅔ jiggers lemonade
Lemon slice
Strawberry

Shake brandy, triple sec and lemonade with ice and strain into a wine goblet over ice. Garnish with a lemon slice and strawberry. Makes 1 drink.

ZOOM

1½ jiggers California brandy
⅓ jigger honey
½ jigger cream

Shake with ice and strain into a cocktail glass.
Makes 1 drink.

BRANDIED PEACH FIZZ

1 jigger California brandy
⅓ jigger peach brandy
⅓ jigger lemon juice
½ teaspoon sugar
½ tablespoon crème de banana
Soda water
Peach slice

Shake brandies, lemon juice, sugar and crème
de banana with ice and strain into a tall
glass. Fill with ice and soda water, then add
peach garnish. Makes 1 drink.

GRAND APPLE

1 jigger apple brandy
⅓ jigger Grand Marnier
⅓ jigger California brandy
Lemon twist
Orange peel

Stir well with ice and strain into a cocktail
glass. Add fruit garnish. Makes 1 drink.

*President John Adams personally concocted a
Berry Shrub using 2 cups blackberry juice,
½ cup sugar dissolved in hot water and 1 cup
brandy and rum. Thank you, John Adams.*

Coolers

Coolers are American in origin. Some people think that they are long cocktails, but I disagree. Coolers probably got their name from the South, since they are often served in tall glasses that are always pictured with pearls of water slipping down the sides of the glasses. In the cooler family are the mists, fizzes, cobblers, rickeys, slings and some single-serving punches. In addition, you can compound your own special cooler and even name it after you or your wife. But make sure it has California brandy.

AMBROSIA

⅓ **jigger California brandy**
⅓ **jigger apple brandy**
1 dash triple sec
Juice of 1 lemon
Champagne

Shake all ingredients except champagne well
with ice. Strain over ice cubes into a highball
glass and fill with champagne. Makes 1 drink.

AMERICAN '76

1 jigger California brandy
⅔ **jigger lemon juice**
1 teaspoon sugar
Champagne, iced

Shake brandy, lemon juice and sugar well
with cracked ice. Strain into a 10-ounce glass,
add 2 large ice cubes and fill with champagne. Makes 1 drink.

APPLE BRANDY COOLER

1 jigger California brandy
½ **jigger light rum**
2 jiggers apple juice
¼ **jigger dark rum**
Lime slice

Shake brandy, light rum and apple juice with
ice. Strain into a tall glass, then fill with ice.
Float dark rum on top and add lime garnish.
Makes 1 drink.

B & B COLLINS

1 jigger California brandy
⅔ jigger lemon juice
1 teaspoon sugar
Soda water
Benedictine
Lemon wedge

Shake brandy, lemon juice and sugar well
with ice. Strain into a tall glass, then fill with
ice and soda water. Float desired amount
of Benedictine on top and add lemon wedge.
Makes 1 drink.

BACHELOR'S BLUSH

½ cup crushed ice
1 jigger California brandy
⅔ jigger lemon juice
⅓ jigger simple syrup
½ jigger triple sec or Cointreau
⅓ jigger grenadine
⅓ jigger apricot brandy
Maraschino cherry
Lemon or lime slice

Whirl all ingredients execpt fruit in blender
until smooth. Serve over crushed ice in 15-
ounce glass. Garnish with cherry and lemon
or lime slice and small umbrella, if desired.
Makes 1 drink.

BATH CURE

⅔ jigger lemon juice
⅔ jigger pineapple juice
⅓ jigger grenadine
1 jigger dark rum
⅔ jigger light rum
⅔ jigger vodka
1 jigger California brandy
⅓ jigger 151 proof rum

Shake or blend well with ice and strain into a
tall glass. Makes 1 drink.

BITTER BRANSHER

⅔ jigger California brandy
⅔ jigger cream sherry
⅓ jigger lemon juice
½ tablespoon Cherry Heering
Bitter lemon soda
Lemon twist

Shake California brandy, cream sherry, lemon
juice and Cherry Heering with ice and strain
into a tall glass. Fill with ice and bitter lemon
soda, then add lemon twist. Makes 1 drink.

BONANZA

⅔ jigger California brandy
1 jigger sherry
Riesling wine

Pour California brandy and sherry into a
highball glass. Fill with ice and wine. Makes 1
drink.

BRACER HIGHBALL

1 jigger California brandy
½ tablespoon anisette
1 dash angostura bitters
½ teaspoon sugar
⅓ jigger lemon juice
1 egg
Soda water

Shake all ingredients except soda well with ice and strain into a highball glass. Fill with ice and soda water. Makes 1 drink.

BRANDIED BANANA COLLINS

1 jigger California brandy
⅔ jigger crème de banana
⅔ jigger lemon juice
Soda water
Lemon wedge
Banana slice

Shake California brandy, crème de banana and lemon juice with ice and strain into a tall glass. Fill with club soda water and ice. Garnish with lemon wedge and banana slice. Makes 1 drink.

Presidents borrowed from one another. Zachary Taylor often served a special wine jelly made with sherry, brandy and garnished with whipped cream and fresh fruit. It appeared on President Taylor's menu as Thomas Jefferson's Wine Jelly.

BRANDIED CHERRY CIDER

2 jiggers cherry cider or cherry juice
1⅓ jiggers apple juice
1 jigger California brandy
Fresh fruit slices

Combine cherry cider, apple juice and brandy
in an 8-ounce glass. Add ice cubes, stir and
garnish with fresh fruit slices. Makes 1 drink.
May also be prepared in a 1 or 2-quart
pitcher. Simply increase measures according
to number of guests being served and garnish
with fresh citrus slices.

BRANDY AND BITTER LEMON

1 jigger California brandy
Bitter lemon, iced

Pour California brandy over ice into a tall
glass. Fill with bitter lemon. Makes 1 drink.

BRANDY BERRY FIX

1 teaspoon sugar
1⅓ jiggers California brandy
½ tablespoon strawberry liqueur
½ jigger lemon juice
Lemon wedge
Strawberries

Into a highball glass pour brandy, liqueur,
lemon juice and sugar dissolved in a little
water. Fill with crushed ice. Stir, then add
lemon and strawberry garnishes. Makes 1
drink.

BRANDY BUCK

1 jigger California brandy
⅓ jigger lemon juice
Ginger ale
Lemon twist

Combine California brandy and lemon juice
in a highball glass. Fill with ice and ginger ale.
Add lemon twist. Makes 1 drink.

BRANDY COLLINS

1⅔ jiggers California brandy
1 to 2 teaspoons sugar
⅓ to ⅔ jiggers lemon juice
Club soda, iced
Lemon slice
Orange slice
Maraschino cherry

Shake brandy, sugar and lemon juice well
with ice. Strain into a 14-ounce glass half
filled with ice. Add soda and stir. Garnish with
fruit. Makes 1 drink.

BRANDY FIZZ

2 jiggers California brandy
1 tablespoon powdered sugar
Juice of ½ lemon
Juice of ½ lime
Soda water

Shake well with ice and strain into a tall glass.
Fill with soda water. Makes 1 drink.

BRANDY HIGHBALL

1 or 2 jiggers California brandy
Soda water or plain water
Lemon twist

Into a 10-ounce glass place ice cubes and
brandy. Fill with soda water or plain water.
Garnish with a twist of lemon. Makes 1 drink.

BRANDY MINT FIZZ

1 jigger California brandy
½ tablespoon white crème de menthe
½ tablespoon light crème de cacao
1½ tablespoons lemon juice
½ teaspoon sugar
Soda water
Mint sprigs

Shake brandy, crème de menthe, crème de
cacao, lemon juice and sugar with ice. Strain
into a tall glass and fill with soda and ice
cubes. Garnish with mint sprigs. Makes 1
drink.

*Winston Churchill was one of the most noted of
brandy fanciers. He loved brandy and consumed
his share while he was alive. During the historic
Battle of Britain, he vowed to give up brandy
if Hitler successfully invaded England. When the
tide turned, he shouted to his servants at No.
10 Downing, "Brandy, Brandy, Brandy." It must
have been a marvelous night.*

BRANDY MINT JULEP

2 jiggers California brandy
1 teaspoon powdered sugar
4 mint sprigs
Soda water

Fill a tall glass with crushed ice and set it aside. Strip the leaves from 2 sprigs of mint and muddle them in a small glass with the sugar. Add a small splash of soda, muddle again and add the brandy. Stir and strain into the tall glass. Work a long-handled spoon up and down in the mixture until the outside of the glass begins to frost. Decorate with sprigs of mint. Makes 1 drink.

BRANDY RASPBERRY MINT CRUSH

1½ cups pureed, frozen raspberries
½ cup granulated sugar
1 (16-ounce) bottle club soda
¾ cup California brandy
8 fresh mint leaves or 2 tablespoons dried mint leaves
Mint sprigs (optional)

Crush fresh mint in pitcher with a small amount of raspberry puree or add dried mint to the puree mixture. Add sugar, remaining raspberry puree, soda and brandy. Stir and pour over crushed ice in small brandy snifters. Garnish with fresh mint sprig, if available. Makes 4 cups.

Unlike wine, brandy does not deteriorate after being opened. Properly stoppered, it will keep for many months after being opened.

BRANDY SHRUB COOLER

5 lemon rinds
Juice of 7 oranges
5 quarts California brandy
12 cups sugar
1 quart soda water
4 fifths dry sherry

Combine lemon rinds, orange juice and
brandy in a large container and let stand for
five days. Dissolve the sugar in the soda
water, add the sherry and mix everything well.
Sieve and bottle. TO USE: Put ice in a tall
glass, add 2 ounces of the shrub and fill with
soda or water. Shrub Yield: 9–10 quarts.

BRIGHTON PUNCH

¾ jigger orange juice
⅔ jigger lemon juice
½ jigger bourbon
½ jigger California brandy
½ jigger Benedictine
Soda water
Orange slice
Lemon wedge

Shake juices and liquors well with ice. Strain
into a tall glass and fill with ice and soda
water. Decorate with fruit. Makes 1 drink.

BULL'S EYE

1⅓ jiggers hard cider
⅓ jigger California brandy
Ginger ale

Pour cider and brandy into a highball glass
over ice cubes. Fill with ginger ale and stir.
Makes 1 drink.

BULL'S MILK

1⅓ jiggers California brandy
1⅓ jiggers milk, cold
¼ teaspoon sugar
Nutmeg

Fill highball glass with ice. Add ingredients
and dust with nutmeg. Makes 1 drink.

CALIFORNIA COOLER

1⅓ jiggers California brandy
⅔ jiggers light rum
2 jiggers apple juice
⅓ jigger lime juice
1 teaspoon dark rum
1 slice lime

Shake brandy, light rum, apple juice and lime
juice well with ice. Strain into a tall 14-
ounce glass. Add ice and stir, then float dark
rum on top. Add lime slice.

CALIFORNIA QUAKE

1 jigger California brandy
⅔ jigger lemon juice
1 teaspoon sugar
Champagne, iced

Shake brandy, juice and sugar well with
cracked ice. Strain into a 10-ounce glass. Add
2 large ice cubes and fill with champagne.
Stir very slightly. Makes 1 drink.

CASSISCO

1 jigger California brandy
⅓ jigger crème de cassis
Soda water

Into a highball glass, pour brandy and crème de cassis. Fill with soda water and ice. Stir. Makes 1 drink.

CHAMPAGNE JULEP

4 mint sprigs
1 lump sugar
Water
1 jigger California brandy
Champagne

In a tall glass, crush 4 mint sprigs with a sugar lump and a few drops of water. Fill half the glass with cracked ice, then add 1 jigger California brandy. Fill with champagne and decorate with additional mint sprigs. Makes 1 drink.

CLARET COOLER

2⅔ jiggers red wine
⅓ jigger California brandy
⅓ jigger lemon juice
Soda water
⅓ jigger grenadine or orange curaçao
Lemon twist
Orange peel

Pour wine, brandy and lemon juice into a tall glass. Fill with ice and soda water. Float grenadine or curaçao on top, then add fruit garnish. Makes 1 drink.

COCKTAIL PUNCH

⅔ jigger sherry
⅔ jigger California brandy
⅔ jigger sauterne
Champagne

Into a tall glass pour sherry, brandy and sauterne. Fill with ice, then pour to the rim with champagne. Makes 1 drink.

COFFEE-MINT FRAPPE

1 jigger Kahlua
½ jigger California brandy
⅓ jigger white crème de menthe
⅓ jigger dark crème de cacao
Orange twist

Rub inside of glass with orange twist and fill with crushed ice. Pour in ingredients which have been gently stirred together. Garnish with orange twist. Makes 1 drink.

COLORADO CRUSH

1⅓ jiggers California brandy
½ cup orange juice
⅓ jigger half-and-half (light cream)
⅓ jigger triple sec
Orange juice

Mix for 5 seconds in a blender. Pour over ice in a tall glass and add orange slice. Makes 1 drink.

CREOLE COOLER

1 cup sugar
2 cups lemon juice
1 cup California brandy
2 cups port
3 cups orange juice
1 cup water
Fruit garnish

Mix everything, except fruit garnish, together. Pour into 12 tall glasses half filled with crushed ice. Add garnish. Makes 12 plus coolers.

CURRANT SHRUB

2 cups sugar
2 cups strained currant juice
1 cup California brandy

Mix sugar with juice in a large saucepan and cook 10 minutes, skimming every 3 minutes. When mixture is cool, add brandy. Mix well and bottle. Yield 2 cups.

DIRTY DOG

1 jigger California brandy
Grapefruit juice
⅓ jigger Kahlua (optional)

Into a tall glass pour the brandy. Fill with ice and grapefruit juice. If desired, float Kahlua on top. Makes 1 drink.

DOUBLE-0-7 (007)

⅔ jigger vodka
⅔ jigger California brandy
⅔ jigger bourbon
Orange juice
Squirt or 7-Up
⅔ jigger Ouzo (optional)

Into a tall glass pour vodka, brandy and bourbon. Fill with ice and orange juice. Add 7-Up and Ouzo, if desired. Makes 1 drink.

FOG CUTTER

1½ jiggers light rum
⅔ jigger California brandy
⅓ jigger gin
⅔ jigger orange juice
1 jigger lemon juice
⅓ jigger orgeat syrup
Sherry

Shake all ingredients except sherry with cracked ice and strain into a tall 14-ounce glass. Float sherry on top. Serve with a straw. Makes 1 drink.

FRANK'S REFRESHER

Juice of ½ lemon
1 jigger raspberry syrup
1 jigger California brandy
Champagne, chilled

Pour lemon juice, syrup and brandy over 2 ice cubes in a tall glass. Fill with champagne. Makes 1 drink.

FRENCH 75

Juice of 1 lemon
1 teaspoon sugar
1 jigger California brandy
Champagne, chilled

Shake lemon juice, sugar and brandy well
with ice and strain over ice cubes in a highball
glass. Fill with champagne. Makes 1 drink.

FRENCH 125

¾ jigger California brandy
⅔ jigger sweet-and-sour mix
⅓ jigger soda water
Champagne

Place all ingredients except champagne in a
tall glass with crushed ice. Fill with champagne. Makes 1 drink.

GEORGIA MINT JULEP

1 teaspoon sugar
4 sprigs mint, muddled
1 jigger California brandy
1 jigger apricot brandy
Mint leaves

Into a highball glass place sugar and muddled
mint. Fill with crushed ice, then add brandies.
Stir until glass frosts. Add mint leaf garnish
and serve with a straw. Makes 1 drink.

*Of all the missions founded in California, one
held a great reputation for making exceptional
brandy. It was Mission San Fernando which produced some 2,000 barrels of brandy in the
1830s.*

GOLDEN GATE SUNSET

1⅓ jiggers California brandy
Orange juice, chilled
1 to 2 teaspoons grenadine

Pour brandy over ice cubes into an 8-ounce highball glass. Fill with orange juice, then stir. Add grenadine, but don't stir. Allow it to settle through the drink. Makes 1 drink.

GOLDEN SPIKE

½ cup orange juice
1 jigger 100 proof vodka
⅔ jigger California brandy

Pour into a tall glass and fill with ice. Makes 1 drink.

GREEN AMAZON

⅔ jigger melon-flavored liqueur
⅔ jigger California brandy
⅓ jigger Cointreau
1 dash pineapple juice
1 dash orange juice
1 dash sweet-and-sour mix

Combine ingredients with ice in a blender. Serve in an 11-ounce chimney glass. Makes 1 drink.

It was "guaranteed to make a dancer out of someone who had never even set foot on a dance floor," acclaimed Andrew Jackson. He was referring to a mixture of brandy, champagne, rum, tea, lemon, sugar, and arrack. He named it Daniel Webster Punch. Punch it did!

OVERHAUL

½ jigger California brandy
½ jigger crème de banana liqueur
½ jigger light rum
1 jigger pineapple juice
1 jigger sweet-and-sour mix
1½ cups crushed ice
Lime or lemon slice

Fill a tall 14 to 16-ounce glass with crushed ice. Add ingredients in order given. Garnish with lime or lemon slice. Makes 1 drink.

MY DESIRE

⅔ jigger California brandy
⅔ jigger lemon juice
⅓ jigger simple syrup
⅓ jigger dry vermouth
⅓ jigger blackberry brandy
⅓ jigger crème de noyaux
⅓ jigger Kahlua
½ cup crushed ice
Maraschino cherry
Orange slice

Whirl all ingredients, including crushed ice, in blender until smooth. Serve over additional crushed ice in 16-ounce squall (small hurricane) glass. Garnish with cherry, orange slice and small umbrella, if desired. Makes 1 drink.

Winston Churchill's stomach was upset because he was upset by the troubles in Europe. He had trouble digesting his meals even though he was a guest at the White House by invitation of Franklin Roosevelt. FDR was so concerned about his digestion that he served him champagne and a large snifter of brandy. Churchill's troubles vanished.

HORSE'S NECK
(with a new kick)

1⅓ jiggers California brandy
1 dash bitters
Ginger ale

Into a tall glass place brandy and bitters. Fill
with ice and ginger ale. Makes 1 drink.

HERE'S HOW

1 jigger port
1 jigger California brandy
Jamaica ginger
Soda water
Lemon twist
Nutmeg

Into a highball glass pour port and brandy.
Add ginger to taste. Fill with soda water and
ice. Add lemon twist and sprinkle over top
with nutmeg. Makes 1 drink.

HAVELOCK HIGHBALL

1 jigger California brandy
2 jiggers ginger wine
Soda water
Lemon twist

Pour brandy and wine into a highball glass.
Fill with soda water and ice, then add lemon
twist. Makes 1 drink.

OUZO RICKEY

⅔ jigger Ouzo
⅔ jigger California brandy
⅔ jigger lime juice
Soda water

Combine Ouzo, brandy and lime juice in a
highball glass. Leave the lime shell in the glass
and fill with soda water and ice. Makes 1
drink.

PARACHUTE COOLER

⅔ jigger California brandy
⅔ jigger Kirschwasser
⅔ jigger coffee
1 egg white
Soda water

Shake all ingredients except soda water well
with ice and strain into a tall glass. Fill with ice
and soda water. Makes 1 drink.

PEACH FIZZ

1 jigger California brandy
1 jigger peach brandy
2 teaspoons lemon juice
2 teaspoons Benedictine
Soda water
Peach garnish

Shake brandies, lemon juice and Benedictine
well with ice and strain over cracked ice into a
tall glass. Fill with soda water and garnish
with fresh or brandied peach. Makes 1 drink.

PETRIFIER

⅔ jigger **California brandy**
⅔ jigger **gin**
⅔ jigger **vodka**
⅔ jigger **triple sec**
⅔ jigger **grenadine syrup**
⅓ jigger **Grand Marnier**
2 dashes **bitters**
Ginger ale
Lemon slices
Orange slices
Maraschino cherry

Pour brandy, gin, vodka, triple sec, grenadine, Grand Marnier and bitters over ice in a 27-ounce magna grande glass. Fill with ginger ale. Thread fruit on a wooden skewer and float in drink. Serves 6.

PICON PUNCH

1 jigger **Amer Picon**
½ tablespoon **grenadine**
Soda water
⅓ jigger **California brandy**
Lemon twist

In a highball glass combine Amer Picon and grenadine. Fill with soda water and ice. Float brandy on top, then add lemon twist. Makes 1 drink.

When author Lucius Beebe was asked what he would do if he got stranded in the Swiss Alps, he answered he would require the services of two St. Bernards, one with the brandy and one with the crème de menthe, so he could make stingers to weather the storm.

PINEAPPLE LEMONADE

2 pineapple pieces
1 teaspoon sugar
1 dash grenadine
1 jigger California brandy
⅔ jigger lemon juice
Soda water
Pineapple spear
Lemon twist

In a tall glass muddle pineapple pieces with sugar and grenadine. Add brandy and lemon juice. Fill with ice and soda water, then add fruit garnish. Makes 1 drink.

POLYNESIAN HURRICANE

½ jigger gin
⅔ jigger California brandy
½ jigger apricot brandy
⅔ jigger rum
1 jigger pineapple juice
1 jigger orange juice
1 jigger lemon juice
1 teaspoon sugar

Shake well with ice and strain into a double old-fashioned glass. Makes 1 drink.

RUSSIAN PUNCH

⅔ jigger California brandy
⅔ jigger Kummel
Champagne

In a highball glass combine brandy and Kummel. Fill with champagne and ice. Makes 1 drink.

PORT WINE SANGAREE

2 jiggers port wine
½ jigger California brandy
1 teaspoon superfine sugar
1 teaspoon lemon juice
Splash of soda water
Stout
Nutmeg

Pour wine, brandy, sugar and lemon juice into
a highball glass. Stir, then fill with ice. Add
splash of soda water and float stout on top.
Dust with nutmeg. Makes 1 drink.

PROVINCETOWN

1 jigger California brandy
½ jigger cranberry liqueur
1 dash orange bitters
Bitter lemon with quinine
Lime slice

Pour brandy, cranberry liqueur and bitters
over ice cubes in a highball glass. Fill with bitter lemon, then garnish with lime slice. Makes
1 drink.

REVIVER COOLER

1 jigger California brandy
⅓ jigger framboise liqueur
2 jiggers milk, cold
Soda water

Shake brandy, liqueur and milk well with ice
and strain into a highball glass. Fill with soda
water. Makes 1 drink.

SCHUSSBOOMER'S DELIGHT

½ jigger lime juice
1 jigger California brandy
Champagne

Into a tall glass pour lime juice and brandy.
Fill with champagne and ice. Makes 1 drink.

SCORPION

½ cup shaved ice
1½ jiggers light rum
1 jigger California brandy
⅔ jigger lemon juice
⅔ jigger orange juice
1 teaspoon orgeat syrup
1 teaspoon 151 proof rum
Gardenia blossom

Place all ingredients except 151 proof rum in
blender and blend 10 seconds. Pour into
grapefruit supreme glass and float 151 proof
rum on top. Garnish with gardenia blossom if
available. Makes 1 drink.

SHERRY COBBLER

½ teaspoon sugar
⅔ jigger California brandy
⅓ jigger orange juice
1⅔ jiggers sherry
Orange slice

Combine ingredients in a tall glass. Fill with
crushed ice and garnish with an orange slice.
Makes 1 drink.

SINGAPORE SLING

⅔ jigger lime juice
⅔ jigger cherry liqueur
1⅓ jiggers gin
Soda water
4 drops California brandy
4 drops Benedictine
Orange slice
Mint sprig

Shake lime juice, liqueur and gin well and pour over ice cubes in a tall glass. Fill with soda water, then decorate with an orange slice and mint sprig. Add the brandy and Benedictine through the middle with a dropper. This recipe is the original from the Raffles Hotel in Singapore. Makes 1 drink.

ST. CROIX COOLER

1⅓ jiggers rum
⅓ jigger dark rum
⅔ jigger California brandy
1 teaspoon brown sugar
1⅔ jiggers orange juice
1 jigger lemon juice
1 dash orange flower water
Squirt (grapefruit) soda

Shake all ingredients except soda water well with ice and strain into a tall glass. Fill with Squirt and ice. Makes 1 drink.

How old is brandy? No one knows. There are references in ancient Arabic to a spirit distilled from wine as early as the 12th Century. Brandy has become so popular a drink today that virtually every major wine producing country in the world makes brandy.

SUMMER TOM & JERRY

⅓ cup crushed ice
1 jigger California brandy
⅔ jigger light rum
⅓ jigger lemon juice
1 egg yolk
1½ teaspoons sugar

Blend all ingredients at low speed for 20 seconds. Pour into a chilled champagne glass. Makes 1 drink.

VANILLA PUNCH

1 jigger California brandy
⅔ jigger crème de vanille
⅓ jigger lemon juice
Sugar to taste
Soda water

Shake all ingredients except soda water with ice and strain over ice cubes into a tall glass. Fill with soda water. Makes 1 drink.

WHITE WINE COOLER

⅓ jigger California brandy
⅓ jigger Kümmel
⅓ jigger lemon juice
1 teaspoon sugar
1 dash orange bitters
White wine, chilled

Into a tall glass pour all ingredients except wine. Fill with ice and chilled wine. Makes 1 drink.

Punches
and
Holiday Nogs

There are literally thousands of recipes for punch, that thirst quencher par excellence. Huge punch bowls filled with a variety of imaginative ingredients have long been a part of our heritage. They make almost any occasion festive.

Punch is believed to have originated with those fiesty English sailors. The largest punch ever prepared and recorded was devised by an English sea captain who wanted to subdue the parched palates of some 6,000 of his guests. Here's his recipe:

80 casks of brandy
9 casks of water
25,000 large limes
80 pints of lemon juice
1,300 pounds of sugar
5 pounds of nutmeg
1 cask of Malaga wine

He poured all the ingredients into a large marble basin. To serve his guests, small boys used a rowboat floating on that vast alcoholic sea, but the fumes overcame them and they had to be replaced every 15 minutes.

"Nogs" are the short-end expression for eggnogs, those sweet delightful drinks that are so popular with the ladies. It is too bad that "nogs" aren't served more often throughout the year instead of just during the holiday season.

And so we present an honored collection of the best punches and nogs which we hope will please your palate.

BACHELOR PARTY CHEER

1 cup sugar
1 cup lemon juice
1 cup California brandy
1 cup 151 proof rum
1 cup golden rum
3 fifths California sparkling red wine, chilled

Dissolve the sugar in the lemon juice. Add brandy and the two rums. Chill. When ready to serve, pour the brandy-rum mixture into a punch bowl, add block of ice and pour in the sparkling red wine. Serves 12.

Ever hear of or taste Cherry Bounce? Blend five pints of fresh, mashed and strained cherries to every quart of brandy. To every gallon of the mixture add three quarters of a pound of brown sugar. This was the family recipe of George Washington.

BALTIMORE EGGNOG

12 eggs, separated
1 pound powdered sugar
2 cups California brandy
1 cup light rum
1 cup peach brandy
6 cups milk
2 cups heavy cream

Beat egg yolks with sugar. Slowly stir in brandies, rum, milk and cream. Chill thoroughly, then fold in stiffly-beaten egg whites before serving. Makes 25 to 30 cups.

BELLEVUE EGGNOG

12 eggs, separated
Sugar to your taste
2 cups California brandy
1 cup rum
2 cups milk
1 cup cream
Ground nutmeg

Beat egg yolks gradually adding the sugar. Add brandy, rum, milk and cream. Mix well. Beat egg whites until they hold their peaks and fold into yolk mixture. Pour mixture into a punch bowl and dust the top with ground nutmeg. Serves 12.

California brandy is a natural grape product produced from the Thompson, Tokay, Emperor, Grenache, Columbard, Malaga, Petite Sirah and St. Emilion grapes. The difference in the brandies is the secret in the brandymasters skill of the final blend. Taste, Taste, Taste!

BOMBAY PUNCH

4 cups California brandy
4 cups sherry
½ cup maraschino liqueur
½ cup orange curaçao
2 fifths champagne
1 fifth carbonated water
Fruit garnish
Cracked ice

Pour all ingredients in a large punch bowl and
stir gently. Let chill for ½ hour. Yield 32 cups.

BOSTON EGGNOG

1 egg yolk
¾ teaspoon sugar
1 teaspoon California brandy
½ teaspoon dark rum
½ cup Madeira wine
Milk
Nutmeg

Beat egg yolk and sugar. Add to brandy, rum
and wine. Shake well with ice and strain
into a tall glass. Fill with milk and ice. Dust
with nutmeg. Serves 2.

*Never heat brandy with a flame. Nothing ruins
the exquisite taste of a California brandy more
than heating the spirit in a brandy snifter. Let the
warmth of your hand seep upward through the
bowl of the snifter, allowing you to experience
the skill of the brandymaster as the perfume
caresses your senses.*

BRANDY BRUNCH PUNCH

2 peaches, pared and thickly sliced
3 apricots, halved
3 plums, halved
12 strawberries, hulled and halved
2 tablespoons sugar
2 cups California brandy
**2 cups champagne or sparkling water,
chilled**

Place chilled fruit pieces in 1½ to 2-quart
pitcher. Add sugar and pour in brandy. Stir
gently, cover and refrigerate 1 hour. Just before serving, add champagne or sparkling
water. Serve in chilled glasses or over ice.
Makes about 3½ cups. Retain fruit pieces to
serve with brunch. Serves 6.

Note: If lighter beverage is desired, double
champagne or sparkling water.

BRANDY EGGNOG

12 eggs, separated
½ cup sugar
12 cups milk
1 cup heavy cream
1 fifth California brandy
½ cup rum
Nutmeg

Beat yolks and sugar. Add remaining ingredients except egg whites. Refrigerate. Before
serving, fold whites into mixture and dust with
nutmeg. Serves 12.

BRANDY MILK PUNCH

1 jigger California brandy
1 jigger dark crème de cacao
1 teaspoon sugar
Few drops vanilla extract
2⅔ jiggers half-and-half (thin cream)
Nutmeg

Whirl all ingredients except nutmeg in
blender. Pour over ½ cup ice in a 13-ounce
stemmed glass. Sprinkle with nutmeg. Makes
1 drink.

BRANDY PUNCH BOWL

1⅓ cups granulated sugar
12 oranges
Block of ice (small)
1 fifth Burgundy
1 fifth ruby port
1 fifth California brandy
4 cups club soda

In a large bowl dissolve the sugar in the juice
of 6 of the oranges. Add block of ice along
with Burgundy, port, brandy and club soda.
Garnish with half slices of remaining oranges.
Serve in punch cups. Serves 25.

CALIFORNIA EGGNOG

1¼ teaspoons California brandy
1¼ teaspoons bourbon
1½ teaspoons rum
1 egg
2 teaspoons cream
Nutmeg

Shake well with ice and strain into a tall glass.
Sprinkle nutmeg on top. Makes 1 drink.

CARDINAL PUNCH

1½ pounds sugar
Juice of 12 lemons
4 cups soda water
8 cups claret or other red wine
2 cups rum
1 cup sweet vermouth
2 cups California brandy
2 cups champagne
Block of ice
Fruit garnish (pineapple and orange
  slices)

Dissolve sugar in lemon juice. Add other ingredients except champagne and fruit. Chill.
To serve place in punch bowl with ice block.
Add champagne and decorate with fruit as
desired. Makes 34 4-ounce servings.

CHAMPAGNE CUP

Ice cubes
1 orange, sliced
1 lemon, sliced
1 lime, sliced
1 jigger maraschino liqueur
1 jigger green Chartreuse
1 jigger California brandy
1 jigger orange curaçao
1 fifth champagne

Fill 3-quart pitcher quarter full with ice cubes.
Add all ingredients except champagne. Stir,
then refrigerate for 1 hour. Fill pitcher with
champagne, then pour into champagne
glasses. Serves 6.
  Note: We know of five versions of Champagne Cup. Other versions add: pineapple
spears, Grand Marnier, Benedictine and mint
sprigs.

CHAMPAGNE PUNCH

Juice of 12 lemons
Sugar to taste
Block of ice
1 cup maraschino liqueur
1 cup orange curaçao
2 cups California brandy
2 cups soda water
8 cups champagne

Sweeten lemon juice with sugar to taste. Add to punch bowl with block of ice, then pour in remaining ingredients. Makes 28 4-ounce servings.

Note: More than six versions of this delicious punch exist. One version substitutes powdered sugar and water for the sweetened lemon juice. Another substitutes Cointreau for the curaçao. Still another specifies yellow Chartreuse instead of curaçao. While another recommended adding 1 cup of strawberries or raspberries to the mix. Our final discovery recommended orange bitters for the curaçao.

Ever hear of "Lodi Scotch"? It is made from the Flame Tokay grape and produces a California brandy with a special and distinctive aroma and light body. The Lodians gave it its name of Lodi Scotch. It's great.

CIDER CUP

Cider, of course, refers to the one and only apple cider. It is not well known but apple cider is a product of Normandy, one of the most northern areas in France. The Normans are known for their apple trees, milk, cream and butter. They drink great quantities of apple cider and from it make their famous brandy, Calvados, a first cousin to California brandy. These Normans are blessed with the tastes of their exceptional butter on hot French bread, their cream in coffee and their milk on fresh cinnamon baked apples.

Cider is one of the most acceptable drinks in the United States. And when blended with mellow California brandy, it becomes a Norman conquest!

Ice cubes
6 pieces each of lemon and orange peel
4 cups apple cider
1 jigger maraschino liqueur
1 jigger orange curaçao
1 jigger California brandy
Soda water

Mix altogether in a large pitcher. Serves 6.

Note: Alternate versions recommend substituting apple brandy or triple sec for maraschino.

*It is often referred to as America's "brandyland."
It's name is the San Joaquin Valley.*

CLARET CUP

4 teaspoons powdered sugar
¾ cup soda water
⅓ jigger orange curaçao
⅓ jigger triple sec
1⅓ jiggers California brandy
Claret or any red wine
Mint sprigs

In a large pitcher dissolve sugar in soda water.
Pour in curaçao, triple sec and brandy. Add
ice cubes, then fill with claret. Decorate with
mint sprigs. Serves 6.

CLUBHOUSE PUNCH

1 pineapple, peeled, cored and sliced
   thin
3 lemons, sliced thin
Powdered sugar
Cake of ice
1 fifth California brandy, chilled
1 fifth sherry, chilled
1 fifth Sauterne, chilled
2 fifths champagne, chilled

In a large punch bowl, put in the pineapple
and lemon slices and sprinkle with powdered
sugar. Let stand for 2 hours. Add the cake
of ice and remaining ingredients. Yield: 20 6-
ounce servings.

If you like brandy, thank the Dutch merchants.
They took wine and eliminated the water which
allowed them to transport more wine through
the spirit. The drink became so popular that
a brandy trade developed.

DRAGOON PUNCH

1 cup sugar syrup
1 cup sherry
1 cup California brandy
6 cups port
6 cups ale
6 cups champagne
3 lemons, sliced thin

In a punch bowl mix ingredients except
champagne and add ice block. Before serving
pour in champagne and decorate with lemon
slices. Yield: 40 4-ounce servings.

EGGNOG

12 eggs, separated
1 pound powdered sugar
2 cups dark rum
2 cups California brandy
2 cups light rum
8 cups half-and-half (thin cream)
1 cup apricot brandy
Grated nutmeg

Beat yolks until light, then beat in powdered
sugar. Add 2 cups dark rum and beat well.
Refrigerate 2 hours. Add brandies and rum.
Chill until needed. Just before serving, beat
egg whites to soft peaks and fold into cream.
Combine with chilled yolk-liquor mixture.
Pour into punch bowl and sprinkle with
freshly grated nutmeg. Serves 24.

*Today, most of us begin our day with a glass of
juice: orange, grapefruit, pineapple, etc. In the
colonial days, many a planter would begin his
day with a glass of punch: a mixture of brandy,
rum and a few spices.*

FISH HOUSE PUNCH

Fish house punch was a favorite beverage in colonial America

1½ cups superfine sugar
1 bottle dry white wine
2 cups lemon juice
1 fifth dark rum
1 fifth golden rum
1 fifth California brandy
1½ cups peach brandy
1½ cups apricot brandy

Heat sugar, wine and lemon juice and stir well. Add remaining ingredients and let stand at room temperature 3 hours. Chill well. Pour into punch bowl and add peach ice ring. Serves 24.

Peach Ice Ring: Arrange peach halves in bottom of 6-cup ring mold and garnish with maraschino cherries. Barely cover with water and freeze until solid, at least 24 hours.

GRAPEFRUIT CUP

1 (24 ounce) can grapefruit juice
Segments of 3 large grapefruit
2 ounces grenadine
1 quart California brandy
Block of ice
Mint leaves
2 cups soda water

Pour all ingredients except mint and soda water over ice block in punch bowl. Decorate with mint leaves. Before serving pour in soda water. Yields 10 4-ounce servings.

MENDOCINO EGGNOG

9 eggs, separated
6 tablespoons sugar
4 cups California brandy
1 quart milk
1 jigger rum
1 quart cream, lightly beaten
Grated nutmeg

Beat yolks with sugar. Continue beating slightly, slowly adding brandy, milk, rum and finally cream. Beat egg whites stiffly and add to mixture. Chill in refrigerator for several hours. Serve in punch cups with grated nutmeg on top. Makes about 25 servings.

MINT-ROSÉ CUP

1 lemon, sliced
1 lime, sliced
1 orange, sliced
4 pineapple slices
16 mint sprigs
¼ cup sugar
1 jigger California brandy
1 jigger Grand Marnier
1 jigger maraschino liqueur
1 fifth sparkling rosé wine

Place all ingredients except rosé in 3-quart pitcher. Mull with large spoon, then chill 2 hours. Fill pitcher quarter-full with ice cubes and add rosé just before serving.

NAVY PUNCH

4 pineapples
2 cups sugar
2 cups dark rum
2 cups California brandy
2 cups peach brandy
Juice of 4 lemons
4 quarts champagne, chilled

Mix sliced pineapple with sugar. Add other
ingredients. Chill well. Pour into punch bowl
with block of ice and add champagne. Serves
10.

POIMIROO'S PUNCH

1 large can frozen orange juice
  concentrate
1 small can frozen lemon juice
  concentrate
1 large can pineapple juice
1 liter lemon-lime soda
2 magnums California champagne
2 cups California brandy
Orange slices
Lemon slices
Maraschino cherries

Mix fruit juices together with lemon-lime soda.
Add champagne. Float ice ring made of fruit
juices and cherries. Float California brandy.
Garnish with orange and lemon slices. Yield:
30 4-ounce servings.

QUINTET

Juice of 8 lemons
Juice of 8 oranges
4 fifths white wine
2 jiggers dark rum
2 jiggers California brandy
Block of ice
4 bottles soda water, chilled
Fruit garnish

Combine juices, wine, rum and brandy over block of ice in a punch bowl. When ready to serve fill with soda water. Garnish as desired. Yield: 10 4-ounce servings.

RHINE WINE CUP

1 orange, thinly sliced
1 lime, sliced
Berries, fresh
1 jigger California brandy
1 jigger strawberry liqueur
1 jigger orange curaçao
1 fifth Rhine wine
Cucumber curl (optional)

Place ingredients except wine in 3-quart pitcher and chill at least 2 hours. To serve, fill pitcher half full with ice and pour in wine. Add cucumber garnish if desired. Yield: 6 drinks.

SANGRIA

1 orange, sliced
1 lemon, sliced
1 lime, sliced
2 jiggers California brandy
¼ cup superfine sugar
1 fifth dry red wine
Soda water

Fill 3-quart pitcher quarter-full with ice cubes. Place fruit, brandy, and sugar in bowl and stir. Add wine, then stir and chill 20 minutes. Fill with soda water just before serving. Serves 6.

TEQUILA PUNCH

1 fifth tequila
2 fifths dry white wine
1 cup California brandy
½ cup Cointreau
4 cups pineapple juice
1 fifth champagne

Chill all bottles thoroughly. Just before serving pour all ingredients into punch bowl in order given. Add frozen pineapple ring to keep punch cold. Serves 12.

Even great generals got involved with brandy. One such general was Mariano Guadalupe Vallejo. He was a fierce rival of Agoston Haraszthy and boldly marketed his brandy throughout California. It was reputed to be of excellent quality and taste.

VICTORY COOLER (to go)

1 (6-ounce) can frozen orange juice concentrate
1 (6-ounce) can frozen pineapple-grape-fruit concentrate
⅘ pint California brandy
3 cups water

Turn all ingredients into a ½-gallon portable beverage container half filled with ice cubes, then cover. Take anywhere. When ready to serve, shake well before pouring. Makes about 8 cups.

California brandy is a blend of many different brandies. Some are old, some are young, some are used for their taste, bouquet, balance, lightness, and smoothness, and should be light and soft to the taste. Just think, there are some 200 different brandies you can taste to decide just which one suits your tastes.

Hot Drinks
and
Toddies

You've just conquered that last hill, the perfect "person" said hello, your new job will blow the minds of your friends and right now the whole world is eating out of your hand.

It's toddy time, glogg time, flip time and California brandy time. The perfect drink to celebrate whatever "winner's" circle you have claimed, is made with California brandy. And on cold days, California-inspired hot drinks will favor the thrill for whatever you have in mind. Here's a good starter.

ALHAMBRA ROYAL

½ cup hot chocolate
⅔ jigger California brandy
Fresh grated nutmeg

Pour hot chocolate and brandy into a cup
and dust the top with nutmeg. Stir and serve.
Makes 1 drink.

BLACKBERRY DEMITASSE

⅔ jigger blackberry liqueur
1 tablespoon blackberry jelly
⅔ jigger California brandy
⅔ jigger water
½ tablespoon lemon juice

In a small saucepan heat, but do not boil,
ingredients. Pour into a cup and add a lemon
garnish. Makes 1 drink.

BRANDY APPLE

1⅓ jiggers California brandy
1 cup apple juice
Cinnamon, ground

Heat apple juice and combine with brandy in
a coffee mug. Sprinkle cinnamon over top.
Makes 1 drink.

BRANDY BLAZER

2 jiggers California brandy
1 sugar lump
Orange twist
Lemon twist

Combine ingredients in a small thick glass.
Light with match, stir with long spoon for few
seconds and strain into a cocktail glass. Makes
1 drink.

BRANDY RADIATOR

1⅓ jiggers California brandy
2⅔ jiggers Burgundy
⅓ jigger lemon juice
1 teaspoon sugar
Cinnamon stick
Lemon twist

Combine brandy, Burgundy, lemon juice,
sugar and cinnamon stick in a mug. Heat and
serve with lemon twist. Makes 2 4-ounce
drinks.

*One secret of the great eaters of yesteryear was
to take a snifter of brandy in between eating
those fat and rich courses laden with heavy
sauces. Today, while we are eating much lighter
than our grandparents, it is still a good idea
to sip a little California brandy after a heavy dinner. It's a lot better than Alka-Seltzer.*

CAFE BRULOT

No drink brings more "oh's" and "ah's" than flaming café brulot. Sometimes a restaurant will list it as Cafe Diablo or the "devil's coffee." No matter what you call it, the flaming effect and the taste of the coffee are exceptional. Here is my favorite coffee.

1 cup California brandy
1 one-inch cinnamon stick, crushed
3 tablespoons sugar
10 cloves plus 25 more
1 small piece lemon peel
1 whole orange peel
6 cups strong black coffee

In a deep chafing dish or saucepan add brandy, cinnamon, sugar, 10 cloves and lemon peel. Stud the orange peel with the remaining 25 cloves, about one clove every ¾ inch. Heat the mixture until the brandy sizzles. Ignite. With a long fork, hold the clove-studded orange peel over the flames and with a ladle, pour the flaming brandy up and down the orange peel 5 or 6 times to release the orange oils. Drop the peel into the mixture and add the coffee which will kill the flames. Bring back to hot and serve in cups. Serves 6.

Did you know that the size of the cask in which California brandy is aged makes a difference? There is more exchange between the brandy and the wood in smaller casks than larger ones. All the more reason to taste to please the palate.

CALIFORNIA TODDY

1 teaspoon sugar
1⅓ jiggers California brandy
1 lemon slice
1 cinnamon stick
1 whole clove (optional)

Dissolve the sugar with a little hot water in an 8-ounce tumbler. Add other ingredients and fill with very hot water. Place a spoon in glass to prevent cracking. For parties, multiply quantities by number of servings desired. Makes 1 drink.

GALLIANO TODDY

⅔ jigger Galliano
1 jigger California brandy
½ tablespoon grenadine
Lemon wedge

Into an old fashioned glass pour the Galliano, brandy and grenadine. Fill with hot water. Garnish with the lemon wedge. Makes 1 drink.

GLOGG

½ jigger California brandy
4 jiggers sherry
4 jiggers claret or other red wine
1 teaspoon angostura bitters
¾ cup sugar

Combine all ingredients in a saucepan and bring to sizzling. Put 12 teaspoons in 12 preheated old fashioned glasses and pour the mixture until ¾ full. Some great gloggs are garnished with a raisin and almond in each glass. Serves 12.

HOT BRANDY

This is one of the best and quickest hot brandy refreshers you can serve. It is a perfect cold weather drink.

1 teaspoon sugar
1⅓ jiggers California brandy
Hot water
Ground nutmeg

Put the sugar and brandy into an old fashioned glass. Add hot water, stir to dissolve the sugar and dust with nutmeg. Additional alternative garnish—1 dash cinnamon and lemon twist. Makes 1 drink.

HOT BRANDY FLIP

1 jigger California brandy
1 jigger blackberry brandy
1 small egg lightly beaten
1 teaspoon sugar
1 teaspoon lemon juice
Hot milk
Ground nutmeg

Shake all ingredients in a cocktail shaker except milk. Pour into a mug and fill with hot milk. Dust with nutmeg.

The Sidecar earned its name from a World War I British flying ace, who after a day of battle over the Western front, would ride to a French cafe in a motorcycle sidecar, for his favorite drink.

HOT BRANDY PUNCH

2 lemon peels
¼ teaspoon cinnamon
¼ teaspoon mace
¼ teaspoon cloves
3 cups sugar
1 cup water
Juice of 2 lemons
1 bottle California brandy

Heat all ingredients together in a 2-quart saucepan except lemon juice and brandy. Add these after mixture has reached simmering point. Serves 8.

HOT BRANDY SHRUB

It was Ben Franklin who liked shrub and in 1770 he gave his special recipe to the public. Shrub is a concentrated liquid drink that you can make and bottle for future use. It was a favorite in old England and the American settlers adopted it for their own use. In our recipe below, it is served hot. But on hot days it can be served cold with crushed ice and cold water.

Rind of 5 lemons
Juice of 7 oranges
20 cups California brandy
12 cups sugar
4 cups soda water
12 cups sherry

Mix the first three ingredients and let stand 5 days. Dissolve the sugar in the soda water and add the sherry and mix it with the lemon, orange and brandy mixture. Strain and bottle. To serve hot, pour 2 ounces shrub into a glass and add 5 ounces hot water. Makes 1 drink.

HOT BUTTERED
BRANDY & RUM

1 tablespoon brown sugar batter (recipe below)
⅓ cup boiling water
½ jigger California brandy
½ jigger dark rum
Ground cinnamon to taste

Stir brown sugar batter in the water in an 8 ounce mug. Add remaining ingredients. Makes 1 drink.

BROWN SUGAR BATTER

½ cup butter
1 pound dark brown sugar
1 teaspoon ground cinnamon
1 teaspoon ground clove
½ teaspoon salt

Melt the butter with the brown sugar and when well mixed add the remaining ingredients. Makes enough batter for 32 drinks.

Of all the brandy consumed in the United States, more than 75% of that is California brandy.

HOT BUTTER-SPICED BRANDY

4 cups apple cider
⅓ cup honey or brown sugar
½ teaspoon pumpkin pie spice
  (optional)
½ cup lemon juice
2 cups California brandy
4 teaspoons butter

Combine apple cider, honey or brown sugar, spice and lemon juice in a saucepan and heat to boiling. Measure 1⅓ jiggers brandy and ½ teaspoon butter into each 8-ounce heat-proof mug or glass. Pour in boiling spiced cider and stir gently. Serves 8.

HOT EGGNOG

1 egg
1 teaspoon sugar
⅔ jigger rum
⅔ jigger California brandy
Hot milk
Nutmeg

In a preheated highball glass mix together egg and sugar. Add rum and brandy, then fill with hot milk. Sprinkle nutmeg over top. Makes 1 drink.

HOT BRANDY ORANGE

½ teaspoon sugar
1⅓ jiggers California brandy
Orange peel

Dissolve sugar in a little water. Pour in brandy and flame in glass. Add orange peel. Makes 1 drink.

HOT MILK PUNCH

1 jigger light rum
1 jigger California brandy
1 teaspoon sugar
Hot milk
Nutmeg

Combine the sugar, rum and brandy in a tall glass. Fill with hot milk. Stir and top with nutmeg. Makes 1 drink.

HOT SANGAREE

1 teaspoon sugar
Hot water
1½ jiggers California brandy
Ground nutmeg

In an old fashioned glass, dissolve the sugar in the hot water. Add the brandy, hot water to fill and dust with nutmeg. Makes 1 drink.

HOT TODDY BOWL

1 whole lemon
whole cloves
4 cups California brandy
Sugar syrup to taste
8 cups boiling water
Cinnamon

Stud the lemon with cloves and slice into 16 thin slices. Combine brandy, sugar syrup and lemon slices in a heated bowl. Add boiling water, then ladle into preheated mugs. Float a lemon slice in each and sprinkle cinnamon over top if desired. Serves 16.

LIZARD SKIN

Hollow out half an orange and fill with California brandy. Flame and serve right in orange shell. Serves 1.

TOM & JERRY

This is one of the most treasured recipes in American drinking history. While it is traditionally served during the Christmas holiday season, it can be served anytime and anywhere. There are many variations on the theme, but this one I like best.

1 egg, separated
1 teaspoon brown sugar
¼ teaspoon allspice
1 jigger Puerto Rican rum
1 jigger California brandy
Hot milk

Beat the yolk in a glass bowl with the sugar and allspice. Gradually add the rum and brandy beating the mixture until smooth. Beat the whites until they hold their peaks. Fold whites into yolk mixture. Pour into cup and add hot milk to fill. Makes 1 drink.

It takes 10 casks of good white wine to make one cask of good brandy, which means that brandy can never be cheap.

WASSAIL BOWL

½ cup water
2 pounds sugar
1 teaspoon cinnamon
½ teaspoon mace
6 whole cloves
1 teaspoon nutmeg
2 teaspoons ginger
4 bottles sherry
12 eggs
12 roasted apple slices or 12 tiny
   roasted apples
1 cup California brandy

Mix sugar, cinnamon, mace, cloves, nutmeg
and ginger with water. Add sherry and simmer
over slow fire. Beat eggs separately and add
to hot mixture. To serve, add apples and lace
the mixture with brandy. Yield: 25 4-ounce
drinks.

SETTLER'S PUNCH

1 large orange, quartered
12 whole cloves
2 bottles claret or California red wine
2 cups California brandy
½ cup sugar
4 cinnamon sticks
Orange slices
Lemon slices

Stud the orange quarters with cloves. In a
saucepan combine orange quarters, claret,
brandy, sugar and cinnamon. Cover and simmer about 15 minutes. Remove cinnamon
and orange quarters. Float fruit slices, then ladle hot mixture into small preheated glasses.
Serves 18.

Dessert Drinks

Calorie counting consumers are turning up their noses at heavy desserts and are on the lookout for lighter after-dinner delights. Here is a potpourri of such desserts; light, easy to make and easy on the waistline. Just try this first dessert drink tonight.

BANANA BANSHEE

1 cup crushed ice
1⅓ jiggers California brandy
1 jigger white crème de cacao
½ ripe medium banana
3 teaspoons bar sugar
⅔ jigger light cream
Banana chunk
Strawberry

Whirl all ingredients in blender until well
blended, creamy and frothy. Serve in 12-
ounce stemmed glass. Garnish with banana
chunk and fresh strawberry on pick. Makes 1
drink.

BRANDY ALEXANDER GLACÉ

1 jigger California brandy
⅓ jigger dark crème de cacao
2 scoops vanilla ice cream
Nutmeg

Whirl brandy, crème de cacao and ice cream
in blender. Sprinkle with nutmeg and serve
in an 8-ounce stemmed glass. Makes 1 drink.

BRANDY CAFE

½ cup crushed ice
1 jigger California brandy
1 jigger Kahlua
Whipped cream
Chocolate bits

Whirl in blender and strain into 6-ounce
stemmed cocktail glass. Garnish with whipped
cream and a sprinkling of chocolate bits.
Makes 1 drink.

BRANDY FREEZE

1½ jiggers California brandy
2 scoops coffee ice cream

Blend in blender until smooth, then pour into
a champagne glass. Makes 1 drink.

BRANDY FROSTY FRAPPE

2 cups California brandy
2 cups half-and-half (thin cream)
¼ cup undiluted frozen orange or
**   pineapple juice concentrate**
4 cups orange or pineapple sherbet

Pour brandy and half-and-half into a shallow
pan. Stir to blend, then freeze. When ready to
serve, turn half mixture into chilled blender
jar. Add half the fruit juice concentrate and
sherbet. Blend at high speed. Pour into serving glasses. Repeat with remaining ingredients.
Makes about 10 to 12 servings.

BRANDY ICE

1 jigger California brandy
½ jigger dark crème de cacao
⅔ cup vanilla ice cream
Cinnamon

Whirl brandy, crème de cacao and ice cream
in a blender. Pour into a 6-ounce champagne
glass and sprinkle cinnamon over top. May
also be prepared in large quantities and frozen
in individual glasses. Serve partially or completely thawed. Makes 1 drink.

CHARTREUSECO FRAPPE

⅔ jigger yellow Chartreuse
⅔ jigger California brandy

With finely crushed ice, build a snow cone in a cocktail glass. Pour Chartreuse and brandy over the ice. Serve with short straws. Makes 1 drink.

CHOCOLATE FOG

2 tablespoons instant hot chocolate mix
¾ cup boiling water
1 jigger California brandy
Whipped cream
Chocolate sprinkles

Stir together hot chocolate mix and water in an 8-ounce serving glass or mug. Add brandy. Top with whipped cream and decorate with chocolate sprinkles. Makes 1 drink.

ESKIMO

1⅓ jigger California brandy
½ tablespoon maraschino liqueur
½ tablespoon orange curaçao
⅔ jigger vanilla ice cream

Shake well with ice and strain into a large cocktail glass. Makes 1 drink.

FAT CAT

⅓ **jigger Galliano**
⅓ **jigger white crème de cacao**
⅓ **jigger California brandy**
1 scoop ice cream

Blend with crushed ice and pour into bucket glass. Makes 1 drink.

FROZEN B.C.

⅔ **jigger crème de cassis**
⅔ **jigger pineapple juice**
1 jigger California brandy

Blend ingredients with crushed ice, then build into snow cone in a cocktail glass. Serve with a short straw. Makes 1 drink.

FROZEN BERKELEY

1 jigger rum
⅓ **jigger California brandy**
⅓ **jigger passion fruit syrup**
⅓ **jigger lime juice**

Blend ingredients with crushed ice, then build into a snow cone in a cocktail glass. Serve with a short straw. Makes 1 drink.

One of the best cold remedies is hot lemon, water and one tablespoon of California brandy, plus plenty of sleep.

FROZEN B.P. (Beepe)

1 jigger California brandy
⅔ jigger port
1 egg
1 teaspoon sugar
Grated nutmeg

Blend brandy, port, egg and sugar with
crushed ice, then build into a snow cone in a
cocktail glass. Dust with nutmeg and serve
with a short straw. Makes 1 drink.

FROZEN BRUM

1 jigger California brandy
⅔ jigger gold rum
⅓ jigger lime juice
1 egg yolk
1½ teaspoon sugar

Blend ingredients with crushed ice, then build
into a snow cone in a cocktail glass. Serve
with a short straw. Makes 1 drink.

NEWPORT FLIP

2 jiggers California brandy
1 large egg
2 teaspoons sugar
½ teaspoon instant coffee crystals
½ teaspoon frozen orange juice
    concentrate
Cinnamon

Shake brandy, egg, sugar, instant coffee and
orange juice concentrate well with crushed
ice. Strain into 3-ounce glasses and sprinkle
with cinnamon. Makes 2 drinks.

PATTI DARLING

⅔ jigger California brandy
½ tablespoon Kahlua
⅓ jigger amaretto
⅔ jigger light cream
½ cup bar ice
Almonds, thinly sliced
Cherry (optional)

Whirl all ingredients, except almonds and
cherry, slightly in blender and strain into 4½-
ounce champagne glass. (For more frosty
consistency, blend ice completely and serve in
8-ounce glass.) Garnish with almond slices
and green-stemmed cherry, if desired. Makes
1 drink.

RAZZ-MA-TAZZ

⅔ jigger California brandy
½ jigger raspberry liqueur
⅓ jigger grenadine
¾ cup ice milk
Fruit garnish

Blend in soft ice cream machine to soft ice
cream consistency. Turn into a 6-ounce glass
and garnish with a fresh raspberry or a
stemmed cherry. If a soft ice cream machine is
not available, use a blender. Makes 1 drink.

ROYAL BRANDY ICE

½ cup crushed ice
⅔ jigger California brandy
⅔ jigger dark crème de cacao
1 scoop English toffee ice cream

Whirl all ingredients in blender, then pour into
an 8-ounce stemmed glass. Makes 1 drink.

SEPARATOR

½ jigger Kahlua
⅓ cup heavy cream
½ jigger California brandy

Fill stemmed straight-sided 7-ounce glass with
about 1 cup crushed ice. Add each layer in
order given, being careful not to mix ingredients. Serve with stirrer or straw. Makes 1
drink.

TRIP TO THE MOON

⅔ jigger California brandy
⅓ jigger white crème de cacao
⅓ jigger triple sec
⅓ jigger Galliano
1⅓ cups vanilla ice cream
Mint sprig

Whirl all ingredients until smooth and creamy
in blender. Serve in 10-ounce tulip glass. Garnish with mint sprig. Makes 1 drink.

*Is brandy a popular spirit in the United States?
Well, last year Americans consumed some
140,000 bottles per day. Skoal!*

Coffee and Tea Drinks

Up until about 1945, brandy and coffee drinks were almost unheard of in the best restaurants in the United States. Oh yes, you could always get Café Brulot at Antoine's or Brennen's or Brussard's, where after you order it the house lights would dim and the waiter would ring the bell at the statue of Napoleon. At that moment, all eyes were on you and your table as the head waiter flamed the sizzling coffee and the whole restaurant seemed to light up. But those were rare restaurants.

Today the marriage of coffee and brandy is one of the most celebrated events of the past two decades. It seems that just about every well-known restaurant has some coffee and brandy drink that can be served after dinner. In addition, many restaurants have devised their own special combination of coffee and brandy which has delighted their patrons.

© BILL LANSBERG 1981

Coffee has always been served after the dessert. Brandy has always been served after the coffee when the gentlemen left the room to enjoy their brandy and cigars. That tradition has given way to the more modern practice of men and women enjoying brandied coffee drinks together. And those after-dinner treats take many forms: frappés, punches, flaming coffees, grogs, glaces and some old favorites like Cappucino, Coffee Royal and Hot Brandy Flip.

So let's start off with the Blackjack.

BLACKJACK

1½ tablespoons kirsch
½ tablespoon California brandy
1½ tablespoons coffee

Stir well with ice cubes and strain over crushed ice in a cocktail glass. Makes 1 drink.

BRANDIED COFFEE PUNCH

1 cup coffee grounds
½ teaspoon cardamom seeds
5½ cups boiling water
¾ cup honey
2 cups California brandy

Combine coffee grounds and cardamom seeds in coffee basket of drip or percolator coffee pot. Add boiling water and brew coffee as usual. When coffee is brewed, stir in honey and brandy. Chill thoroughly. When ready to serve, pour over ice in punch bowl. Makes about ½ gallon. Recipe may be increased to make larger quantities as desired.

BRANDY CLASSIC

1⅓ jiggers California brandy
1 large egg
1 teaspoon bar sugar
1⅓ jiggers cold coffee
Nutmeg

Shake brandy, egg, sugar and coffee well with crushed ice. Strain into a 4-ounce glass and sprinkle nutmeg over top. Makes 1 drink.

BRANDY COFFEE BLAZER

2 jiggers California brandy
1 tablespoon honey
1⅓ jiggers hot coffee
Lemon peel

Combine brandy, honey and hot coffee in a mug and mix until honey is dissolved. Pour the blazer into a thick cut glass goblet. Twist the lemon peel over the blazer and drop it into the drink. Makes 1 drink.

BRANDY COFFEE COOLER

1 jigger California brandy
½ cup cold coffee
1 tablespoon cream
1 tablespoon coffee liqueur
1 teaspoon sugar
1 scoop coffee ice cream

Shake brandy, coffee, cream, liqueur and sugar with ice. Strain into a 12-ounce glass and add a scoop of ice cream. Makes 1 drink.

BRANDY CREAM FLIP

2 jiggers California brandy
1⅓ jiggers heavy cream
1 large egg
2 teaspoons sugar
1 teaspoon instant coffee crystals
Sweet chocolate, grated

Shake brandy, cream, egg, sugar and instant coffee well with crushed ice. Strain into 4-ounce glasses and sprinkle with chocolate. Makes 2 drinks.

BRANDY GINGERED COFFEE

1 teaspoon preserved ginger, finely
chopped
½ cup vanilla ice cream
½ cup California brandy
2⅔ cups hot coffee
Preserved ginger syrup

Stir preserved ginger into softened ice cream. Pour 2 tablespoons brandy and ⅔ cup coffee into each 8-ounce cup. Top with about 2 tablespoons ice cream and drizzle a little ginger syrup. Serves 4.

It takes roughly 1 ton of grapes to make 43 proof gallons of brandy.

BRANDY MAPLED COFFEE

2 tablespoons instant coffee crystals
¼ cup maple syrup
½ cup California brandy
3 cups hot milk
Dash cinnamon

Measure 1½ teaspoons instant coffee, 1 tablespoon maple syrup and 1 ounce brandy into
each 8-ounce cup. Pour in hot milk. Stir to
blend and fleck with cinnamon. Makes 4
drinks.

BRANDY ORANGE COFFEE

½ cup California brandy
1⅓ jiggers Grand Marnier
3 cups hot coffee

Measure 2 tablespoons brandy and 1 tablespoon Grand Marnier into each 8-ounce cup.
Add coffee and stir to blend. Serves 4.

BRANDY VELVET

⅔ jigger California brandy
⅔ jigger strong cold coffee
2 tablespoons chocolate syrup
2 scoops coffee ice cream
Chocolate syrup for top

Combine brandy, coffee and chocolate syrup.
Use electric or rotary beater or whirl in
blender with ice cream just until blended.
Pour into an 8-ounce glass and drizzle a little
extra syrup over top. If desired, turn beverage
into pan and freeze until semi-firm, then pile
into a serving glass. Makes 1 drink.

CAFE BRULOT DEMITASSE

8 sugar lumps
6 jiggers California brandy
2 cinnamon sticks, broken
Lemon twist
12 whole cloves
2 orange twists
5 demitasse cups strong black coffee

Place all ingredients except coffee in a chafing dish. Heat gently, stirring constantly with a metal ladle until well warmed. Blaze and let burn about 1 minute. Slowly pour in coffee, then ladle into demitasse cups. Makes 6 drinks.

CAFE DIABLE

2½ cups hot coffee
2 cinnamon sticks, broken
8 whole allspice
4 whole cardamom seeds, shelled
2 teaspoons orange rind, grated
1⅓ jiggers Sambuca
2 jiggers Grand Marnier
⅓ cup California brandy
2 tablespoons sugar

In a chafing dish simmer ½ cup coffee, cinnamon, allspice, cardamom and orange rind. Add the Sambuca, Grand Marnier and brandy. Heat again. When hot, ignite and stir with a long-handled spoon until flame subsides. Then add sugar and remaining 2 cups coffee. Heat and ladle into serving cups. Serves 4.

CAFE CASA ROMERO

1 jigger California brandy
Hot Mexican coffee
1 or 2 teaspoons cream
⅔ jigger Kahlua

Wet rim of 8-ounce glass with brandy, dip in sugar and carmelize in flame. Add warm brandy to preheated glass and flame. Fill to near rim with Mexican coffee (a mixture of coffee, cinnamon and sugar), then add cream and Kahlua. Makes 1 drink.

CAFE GROG

1 jigger light Jamaica rum
1 sugar lump
Lemon wedge
½ tablespoon California brandy
Hot black coffee

Place rum, sugar and lemon in a cup. Add brandy, then fill with coffee. Makes 1 drink.

CALIFORNIA FRAPPE

1 jigger California brandy
1 teaspoon undiluted orange juice
  concentrate
1⅓ jiggers cold coffee
¼ teaspoon bar sugar
Orange slice

Pack finely crushed ice into 8-ounce serving glass. Combine ingredients and pour over ice. Decorate with orange slice. Makes 1 drink.

CAPISTRANO COFFEE

1 jigger California brandy
1 teaspoon chocolate syrup
1 teaspoon brown sugar
¼ teaspoon vanilla
1 dash cinnamon
¾ cup hot coffee
Whipped cream
Cinnamon stick

Stir brandy, chocolate syrup, sugar, vanilla
and cinnamon together in 10-ounce serving
glass or cup. Pour in hot coffee. Top with
whipped cream and add cinnamon stick as a
stirrer. Makes 1 drink.

CAPPUCINO

½ teaspoon sugar
½ teaspoon cocoa powder
1⅔ jiggers strong black coffee
1⅔ jiggers half-and-half (thin cream)
1 jigger California brandy
Whipped cream

Combine sugar and cocoa. Mix with coffee
and half-and-half in an 8-ounce glass. Add
brandy and top with whipped cream. Makes 1
drink.

*In 1769, when the Franciscan Padres founded
Mission San Diego, one of their first chores was
to lay out vineyards to produce wine, and of
course . . . brandy.*

COASTAL SPICED COFFEE

6 cups hot coffee
1 cup California brandy
4 teaspoons granulated sugar
10 to 12 whole cloves
1 orange
6 orange twists

In a saucepan combine coffee, brandy, sugar
and a whole orange studded with cloves.
Warm but do not boil. Serve in preheated
mugs with a twist of orange. Serves 6.

COFFEE CALIFORNIA

½ cup dark brown sugar, packed
2 cinnamon sticks
6 whole cloves
4 cups water
2 tablespoons instant coffee crystals
10 tablespoons California brandy
Brandy cream*

Combine sugar, spices and 2 cups water and
bring to a boil. Lower heat, cover and simmer
5 minutes. Remove cover, add remaining 2
cups water and coffee crystals. Return to
a boil, then strain liquid into serving container.
Pour 1 ounce brandy into each warmed coffee cup. Pour in hot spiced coffee, stir and
top with brandy cream. Do not stir after adding cream. Sip brandied coffee through cream
for true flavor. Serves 5.

Brandy cream—combine 1 cup chilled whipping cream, 1 teaspoon chocolate extract, 1
tablespoon sugar and 1 teaspoon California
brandy in chilled bowl. Beat until stiff. Makes
about 1¾ cups.

COFFEE COCKTAIL

1 jigger California brandy
1 jigger Cointreau
1 jigger cold black coffee

Shake with ice and strain into a cocktail glass.
Makes 1 drink.

COFFEE INTERNATIONAL

⅓ jigger California brandy
⅓ jigger amaretto
Hot coffee
Whipped cream

In a 7-ounce Irish coffee glass, combine
brandy and amaretto. Fill with coffee and top
with whipped cream. Makes 1 drink.

COFFEE NATCHEZ

⅔ jigger California brandy
⅓ jigger dark crème de cacao
Hot coffee
Whipped cream

Combine crème de cacao and brandy in a
coffee cup. Fill with coffee and top with
whipped cream. Makes 1 drink.

For Coffee Natchez Flambé, prepare the
same as for COFFEE NATCHEZ, then rest
flambé spoon of 151 proof rum on the rim of
the cup and flame. Makes 1 drink.

COFFEE NUDGE

⅓ jigger California brandy
⅓ jigger dark crème de cacao
⅔ jigger Kahlua
¾ cup hot coffee
Whipped cream

Combine brandy, crème de cacao and Kahlua in an 8-ounce serving glass or mug. Pour in hot coffee and top with whipped cream. Makes 1 drink. For Coffee Nudge Glace use chilled coffee.

COFFEE SAUSALITO

1 jigger California brandy
2 jiggers cold strong coffee
Soda, iced
Whipped cream
Coffee liqueur

Pour brandy and coffee over ice cubes in a 10 to 12-ounce glass. Fill to near rim with soda. Top with whipped cream and drizzle coffee liqueur. Makes 1 drink.

FIRESIDE COFFEE

1⅓ jiggers California brandy
1 cup hot coffee
Whipped cream
Shaved chocolate

Add the brandy to the coffee, top with whipped cream and dust with shaved chocolate. Makes 1 drink.

GOLDEN EGGNOG

1 jigger California brandy
⅔ jigger coffee liqueur
1 small egg
½ cup half-and-half
1 teaspoon sugar
½ teaspoon instant coffee crystals
Coriander or mace, ground

Shake brandy, liqueur, egg, half-and-half, sugar and instant coffee well with crushed ice. Strain into a 12-ounce glass. Sprinkle lightly with coriander or mace. Serves 1.

HONEY-CREAM COFFEE

½ cup whipping cream
1 tablespoon honey
1 dash cloves
½ cup California brandy
2⅔ cups hot coffee
Cinnamon

Beat cream with honey and cloves until stiff. Pour 1 ounce brandy into each of 4 mugs. Add coffee, top with honey-cream and sprinkle with cinnamon. Serves 4.

A Rickey is any drink made with profuse amounts of lime juice. It was named after Colonel Joe Rickey, who, as the story goes, was neither a colonel nor named Joe.

HOT BRANDY FLIP

1⅓ jiggers California brandy
½ cup port
2 teaspoons sugar
½ teaspoon instant coffee crystals
1 large egg
2 tablespoons heavy cream
Ground nutmeg

Heat brandy, port, sugar and instant coffee together, but do not boil. Beat egg and stir in cream. Slowly pour hot liquid into egg mixture, stirring constantly. Pour into warmed mugs or glasses and sprinkle lightly with nutmeg. Serves 2.

HOT PORT FLIP

2 jiggers port
⅔ jigger California brandy
⅓ jigger coffee
1 egg
1 ounce heavy cream
Nutmeg

Heat port, brandy and coffee. Beat egg until foamy, then stir in cream. Combine mixtures in preheated mug and sprinkle nutmeg over top. Makes 1 drink.

KEOKE COFFEE

½ jigger California brandy
½ jigger Kahlua
Hot coffee
Whipped cream

Pour brandy and Kahlua into coffee mug. Fill to near rim with coffee. Garnish with whipped cream. Makes 1 drink.

MONTEREY MOCHA

⅔ jigger California brandy
⅓ jigger heavy cream
1 teaspoon chocolate syrup or chocolate mint liqueur
1⅓ jiggers cold coffee
Mint sprig

Pack finely crushed ice into an 8-ounce glass. Combine all ingredients and pour over ice. Decorate with mint. Makes 1 drink.

NIKOLOSHKA

1 jigger California brandy
Lemon slice, ⅛ inch thick
Coffee grounds, fresh
Granulated sugar

Trim yellow skin from lemon, leaving a bit of the white rind. Cover one half of the lemon with sugar and the other half with the freshly ground coffee. Fill cordial glass with brandy and sit the lemon slice on rim of glass. Drink the brandy through the lemon. Some Nikoloshka drinkers prefer to chew the wedge as they sip the brandy. Makes 1 drink.

PARISIAN COFFEE

Simply add California brandy and cream to each cup of hot, strong French-roasted coffee.

SAN FRANCISCO FLIP

2 jiggers California brandy
1⅓ jiggers port
1 large egg
2 teaspoons sugar
1 teaspoon instant coffee crystals

Shake all ingredients well with ice and strain into 4-ounce glasses. Makes 2 drinks.

SIERRA TODDY

2 jiggers hot coffee
1 teaspoon brown sugar
1 dash powdered cinnamon
1⅓ jiggers California brandy
Lemon slice, thin

Combine coffee, sugar, cinnamon and brandy in an 8-ounce mug. Stir and add lemon. Makes 1 drink.

Note: If made as a brew to have warm at the bar, substitute 3 whole allspice, 1 whole cardamom crushed for the cinnamon and let mixture blend as it warms.

"What's the best way to enjoy brandy?" asks the lady. "The way you like it," we replied.

23 SKIDOO

2 cups California brandy
2 cups half-and-half
2 tablespoons instant coffee crystals
¼ cup undiluted frozen orange juice concentrate
4 cups orange sherbet

Pour brandy, half-and-half and coffee crystals into a shallow pan. Stir to blend, then freeze. When ready to serve, turn half mixture into chilled blender jar. Add half the fruit juice concentrate and sherbet. Blend at high speed. Pour into serving glasses. Repeat with remaining ingredients. Makes 10 to 12 servings.

VENETIAN COFFEE

1 jigger California brandy
1 cup hot coffee
Sugar to taste
Whipped cream

Add brandy to coffee and sweeten to taste. Top with a float of whipped cream. Makes 1 drink.

If you can taste food, you can taste California brandy. You have some 10,000 taste buds in your mouth. All you have to do is put them to work.

TEA DRINKS

Brandied tea drinks have long been a favorite beverage of Europeans. When the American Revolution was brewing, so were many recipes marrying brandy and tea. And among the most famous marriages of all was Artillery Punch, so named because it was given to the men of the artillery on those cold, lonely nights when the wind whipped through their tattered clothes. There are many recipes for Artillery Punch, but this one will keep the coldest person quite warm.

ARTILLERY PUNCH

4 cups rye whisky
4 cups of claret or any red wine
4 cups strong black tea
2 cups light rum
1 cup of gin
1 cup California brandy
1 jigger Benedictine
2 cups orange juice
1 cup lemon juice
Block of ice

Mix all the ingredients except the ice and allow to stand for several hours. Just before serving, put the block of ice into the punch bowl and pour the mixture over it. Yield: 28 4-ounce servings.

BARBARIAN'S NIP

4 cups strong orange-spiced black tea
4 cups apple juice, unsweetened
3 tablespoons honey
6 3-inch cinnamon sticks
2 cups California brandy
10 strips of orange peel

In a saucepan heat the tea, apple juice, honey and cinnamon sticks. When hot, add brandy and bring to a simmer. Serve in heat-proof glasses and garnish each with a strip of orange peel. Yield: 20 4-ounce servings.

BLACK SHIP TREASURE TEA

3 large eggs
½ cup sugar
1 teaspoon vanilla
Pinch ground cloves
2 cups half-and-half (thin cream)
4 cups strong black tea
1½ cups California brandy
Nutmeg

Beat eggs with sugar, vanilla and cloves until thick and light-colored (about 5 minutes on electric mixer). Combine with half-and-half. Heat tea and brandy to simmering. Pour ½ cup egg base into each heat-proof glass. Fill with hot brandy and tea mixture, then sprinkle with nutmeg. Yield: 8 cups.

BOSTON TEA

1 jigger California brandy
1 cup strong lemon tea
Lemon twist
Sugar to taste
Cinnamon stick (optional)

Pour brandy into a cup and fill with tea.
Sweeten, then garnish with a lemon twist.
Add cinnamon stick if desired. Makes 1 drink.

CHATHAM ARTILLERY PUNCH

1 cup brown sugar
½ cup orange juice
½ cup lemon juice
2 cups tea
2⅔ jiggers whisky
⅔ jigger Benedictine
1⅓ jiggers California brandy
2⅓ jiggers gin
4⅔ jiggers rum
2 cups Catawaba wine or white wine
1 bottle champagne, chilled

Mix sugar with juices and tea. Add remaining
ingredients, except champagne. Mix well,
refrigerate for two days. When ready to serve,
add champagne. Decorate as desired. Yield:
16 4-ounce servings.

CHRISTMAS PUNCH

Christmas is one of the best times to serve punches. They are easy on the hostess because she doesn't have to make special mixed drinks. In addition, there are a variety of foods that can be served with punches and none of them have to be elaborate presentations. Simple hors d'ouevres, canapes, patés and terrines blend well with punches. One lady we know served a simple beef stew and within minutes it was gone.

4 cups strong tea
1 bottle rum
1 bottle rye whisky
1 bottle California brandy
½ bottle Benedictine
1 tablespoon angostura bitters
1 pineapple, peeled and sliced into ½ inch rings
Juice of 12 oranges
½ pound sugar
1 block of ice
2 bottles champagne, chilled

In a large punch bowl combine tea with rum, rye, brandy, Benedictine, bitters and pineapple. Add orange juice and sugar dissolved in a little water. Mix thoroughly. Before serving add ice block and pour in champagne. Yield: 45 4-ounce cups.

COLONIAL TEA PUNCH

Peel of 12 lemons, thinly shaved
Juice of 12 lemons
4 cups strong tea
2 cups sugar
4 cups dark rum
1 jigger California brandy

Place lemon peel in a punch bowl, then add
tea and lemon juice. Mix with sugar and let
stand several hours. Add rum and brandy.
Pour the mixture over crushed ice. Yield: 20
4-ounce servings.

GUARDSMAN'S PUNCH

1 cup California brandy
4 cups Scotch whisky
2 cups green tea
½ cup sugar
⅔ jigger port wine
Lemon twist

Mix all ingredients together and heat in a
large saucepan. When very hot serve in preheated glasses. Yield: 14 4-ounce cups.

NEGRITA GROG

⅓ jigger California brandy
⅓ jigger rum
½ teaspoon sugar
⅓ jigger orange curaçao
⅔ jigger strong tea
Hot water
Lemon wedge

Combine ingredients in an old-fashioned
glass. Fill with hot water and add lemon
wedge. Makes 1 drink.

RHINE WINE PUNCH

12 cups Rhine wine
4 cups soda water, chilled
2½ jiggers California brandy
2½ jiggers maraschino liqueur
1 cup strong tea
½ pound powdered sugar
Fruit garnish

Combine ingredients in a punch bowl set in a bed of crushed ice. Decorate with fruit as desired. Makes 34 4-ounce cups.

SAMURAI SPARKLE PUNCH

12 strawberries, sliced
3 tablespoons sugar
3 cups California brandy
2 small oranges, peeled and cut in wedges
6 cups strong oolong tea
3 tablespoons lemon juice
¼ teaspoon aromatic bitters
1 bottle extra dry champagne or club soda, chilled
Mint sprigs

Mix strawberries with sugar. Add brandy and refrigerate at least 1 hour. Combine orange pieces with tea, lemon, bitters and marinated strawberries. Pour into punch bowl over ice. Gently stir in champagne or soda, then garnish with mint. Makes 28 4-ounce cups.

WILLOW WORLD DREAM TEA

1 lemon
½ teaspoon whole cloves
8 cups strong black tea
½ cup sugar
2½ cups California brandy
Banana slices
Pineapple chunks
Maraschino cherries

Stud lemon with cloves, then peel and slice.
Combine with tea and sugar. Heat, stir in
brandy, then simmer. Skewer fruit pieces on
small picks and place one in each heat-proof
container. Pour in hot brandied tea. Makes 20
4-ounce cups.

Index

Wine Advisory Board Cookbooks

"The Classic Series on Cooking With Wine"

Each book includes its own index; however,
EPICUREAN RECIPES includes a
comprehensive index for the entire cookbook
series. These books are available at
bookstores, wine shops and wineries. If you
have trouble finding them, they may be
ordered direct from The Wine Appreciation
Guild. Also, most other wine books and wine
related items are available.

HOW TO ORDER BY MAIL: Indicate the
number of copies and titles you wish on the
order form below and include your check,
money order, or Mastercard or VISA card
number. California residents include 6% sales
tax. There is a $1.00 shipping and handling
charge per order, regardless of how many
books you order. (If no order form—any
paper will do.) Orders shipped promptly via
U.S. Mail—U.S. & Canada shipments ONLY.

**To order Wine Advisory Board
Cookbooks, please use the order
form on the next page.**

WINE APPRECIATION GUILD ORDER FORM—1377 Ninth Avenue, San Francisco, California 94122

SHIP TO:

Address _____

City _____ State _____ Zip _____

_____ Copies #500 EPICUREAN RECIPES OF CALIFORNIA WINEMAKERS	$5.95@
_____ Copies #501 GOURMET WINE COOKING THE EASY WAY	$5.95@
_____ Copies #502 NEW ADVENTURES IN WINE COOKERY	$5.95@
_____ Copies #503 FAVORITE RECIPES OF CALIFORNIA WINEMAKERS	$5.95@
_____ Copies #504 WINE COOKBOOK OF DINNER MENUS	$5.95@
_____ Copies #505 EASY RECIPES OF CALIFORNIA WINEMAKERS	$5.95@
_____ Copies #640 THE CHAMPAGNE COOKBOOK	$5.95@
_____ Copies #527 IN CELEBRATION OF WINE & LIFE	$9.95@
_____ Copies #554 WINE CELLAR RECORD BOOK	$29.95@
_____ Copies #641 POCKET ENCYCLOPEDIA OF CALIFORNIA WINES	$4.95@
_____ Copies #671 CORKSCREWS	$12.95@
_____ Copies #672 WINE IN EVERYDAY COOKING	$5.95@
_____ Copies #673 CALIFORNIA WINE DRINK BOOK	$3.95@
_____ Copies #721 CALIFORNIA BRANDY DRINK BOOK	$4.95@

California Residents 6% sales tax _____

Plus $1.00 Shipping and handling (per order) $1.00

TOTAL enclosed or charged to credit card _____

Charge to Mastercard or Visa card # _____

Expiration Date _____

Signature _____